THE
ARIZONA
GUN OWNER'S
Guide

Who
can bear arms?

Where
are guns forbidden?

When
can you shoot to kill?

by Alan Korwin
illustrations by Gregg Myers

Bloomfield Press • Phoenix, AZ

ISBN 0-9621958-0-4

ATTENTION Clubs, Organizations, Educators and all interested parties: Contact the publisher for information on quantity discounts! Every gun owner needs this book.

Printed and bound in the United States of America

10   9   8   7

TABLE OF CONTENTS

ACKNOWLEDGEMENTS

This book is really the result of all the help I received, great and small, from the good people who shared their thoughts and resources with me. Thank you.

Landis Aden, Legislative Liaison, Arizona State Rifle and Pistol Association

Terry Allison, President, Arizona State Rifle and Pistol Association

Ben Avery, Arizona Republic columnist, co-author of Arizona's gun laws

Mark Barnett, Community Relations Officer, Scottsdale Police

Bob Cecil, Protection and Compliance Manager, Arizona State Land Department

Bob Corbin, Attorney General, State of Arizona

Nelson E. Ford, Owner, The Gunsmith, Inc.

Howard Gillmore, Assistant Director/Field Services, Parks and Recreation

Lt. Colonel Michael Haran, Staff Judge Advocate, Arizona Army National Guard

Wayne J. Higgins, Criminal Investigator, Bureau of Indian Affairs, Phoenix

Don Jansen, Director, Arizona Legislative Council

Mark Jecker, Public Information Officer, Arizona Game and Fish Department

Wes Keys, Information Coordinator, Arizona Game and Fish Department

Tony Machukay, Executive Director, Arizona Commission on Indian Affairs

Marty Mandall, Owner, Mandall Shooting Supplies, Inc.

Jordan Meschkow, Registered Patent Attorney

Richard B. Oxford, Director, Contract and Records Division, Arizona State Land Department

Mary Peterson, NRA Representative

Ron Peterson, Inspector, Bureau of Alcohol, Tobacco and Firearms, Phoenix Branch

Ruth Peterson, Secretary to the Forest Supervisor, U.S. Forestry Service

Bob Reyes, Park Operations Specialist, National Parks Service

Robert J. Spillman, Attorney at Law

Paul Stearns, Police Officer, Scottsdale Police Department

Deborah Stevens, Public Affairs Specialist, Bureau of Land Management

Russell Vanden Wolf, Inspector, Bureau of Alcohol, Tobacco and Firearms, Phoenix Branch

Ken Wagner, Chief of Operations Section, Arizona State Parks

Pete Weinel, Assistant Recreation/Wilderness Staff, U.S. Forest Service

This list would be incomplete without the friends who have been supportive, informative, and whose time and thoughts made a real difference: Harvey and Eileen Barish, Linda Brott, Steve Cascone, Crosby!, Candice DeBarr, Adam Mohney, Gregg Myers, Bill Plummer, Curt Prickett, Dan and Mary Sharayko, Pete Slater, Mary Westheimer and Howard White.

The National Rifle Association Institute allowed the use of material in their pamphlet, "Your State Firearms Laws".

Illustrations by Gregg Myers
Book design by Ralph Richardson
Edited by Howard White
Proofread by The Wordsmith
Typesetting by Mesa Graphics, Inc.
Digital disk transfers by Code Busters

PREFACE

Arizona has strict gun laws. You have to obey the laws. There are serious penalties for breaking the rules.

Many gun owners don't know all the rules. Some have the wrong idea of what the rules are.

Here at last is a comprehensive book, in plain English, of the laws and regulations which control firearms in Arizona.

FOREWORD

DON'T MISS THIS !

This book is not a substitute for the law. In explaining the general meanings of the laws, using plain English, differences inevitably arise. You are fully accountable under the exact wording and current interpretations of all applicable laws and regulations when you deal with firearms under any circumstances.

This book describes the gun laws as they apply to law-abiding private residents in the state of Arizona. It is not intended to and does not describe most situations relating to licensed gun dealers, museums or educational institutions, local or federal military personnel, American Indians, foreign nationals, the police or other peace officers, any person summoned by a peace officer to help in the performance of official duties, persons with special licenses (including collectors), persons with special authorizations or permits, bequests or intestate succession, persons under indictment, felons, prisoners, escapees, government employees, or other people prohibited from firearm possession.

The main relevant parts of Arizona state criminal laws which relate to guns are reproduced in Appendix D. These are formally known as *Arizona Revised Statutes, Title 13, Criminal Code*. Certain other state laws which may apply in some cases, such as Hunting Laws and official agency regulations, are discussed but the laws are *not* reproduced. Key federal laws are discussed, but the laws themselves are *not* reproduced. Case law decisions, which effect the interpretation of the statutes, are *not* included.

Firearms laws are subject to change. You are strongly urged to consult with a qualified attorney and local authorities to determine the current status and applicability of the law to specific situations which you may encounter. A list of the proper authorities appears in Appendix C.

• • • • • • • •

Many people find laws hard to understand, and gathering all the relevant ones is a lot of work. This book helps you with these chores. Collected in one volume are the principal laws controlling gun use in Arizona.

In addition, the laws and other regulations are expressed in regular conversational terms for your convenience. While great care has been taken to accomplish this with a high degree of accuracy, the explanatory sections of this book are not to be considered as legal advice or a restatement of law. The author and publisher expressly disclaim any liability whatsoever arising out of reliance on information contained in this book. New laws and regulations may be enacted at any time by the authorities. The author and publisher make no representation that this book includes all requirements and prohibitions which exist.

A WORD TO THE WISE

Guns are serious business and require the highest level of responsibility from you. What the law says and what the authorities and courts do aren't always an exact match. You must remember that each legal case is different and frequently lacks prior court precedents. A decision to prosecute a case and the charges brought may involve a degree of discretion from the authorities involved. Sometimes, there just isn't a plain, clear-cut answer you can rely upon. **ALWAYS ERR ON THE SIDE OF SAFETY**.

To my wife Cheryl,
my daughter Tyler,
my brother Richard,
and my parents.

THE RIGHT TO BEAR ARMS 1

In the United States of America, citizens have always had the right to bear arms. The Second Amendment to the United States Constitution is the foundation of this right to have and use guns. The Second Amendment is entitled *The Right To Keep And Bear Arms*. This is what it says:

> "A well regulated Militia, being necessary to the security of a free State, the right of the people to keep and bear Arms, shall not be infringed."

The intentions of the revolutionaries who drafted the constitution were clear at the time. It was this right to bear arms which allowed those citizens 200 years ago to break away from British rule. An armed populace was a precondition for independence and freedom. The founders of the United States of America wanted it to stay that way:

> "No free man shall be debarred the use of arms."
> **- Thomas Jefferson**

> "The Constitution shall never be construed to authorize Congress to prevent the people of the United States, who are peaceable citizens, from keeping their own arms." **- Samuel Adams**

> "Little more can reasonably be aimed at with respect to the people at large than to have them properly armed." **- Alexander Hamilton**

"Americans have the right and advantage of
being armed."   **- James Madison**

"The great object is that every man be armed.
Everyone who is able may have a gun."
                              - Patrick Henry

Today the issue is controversial and emotionally charged.
There are powerful and vocal groups on all sides of the
topic of guns. The Supreme Court has been mostly quiet
on the subject, in particular refraining from comment on
the meaning of the "Militia" clause in the Second
Amendment.

Nothing in Arizona law may conflict with the U.S.
Constitution, and so the right to bear arms is passed
down to Arizonans, as it is to the citizens of all the states
in the union. The states, however, pass laws to organize
and control the arms which people bear within their
borders. That's what this book is about.

The majority of the Arizona "gun laws" are in a book
called, *Arizona Revised Statutes, Title 13, Criminal Code.*
It is widely available in libraries, and a copy may be
obtained inexpensively from the Secretary of State's
office. The main relevant sections of the law are printed
in Appendix D. Many of the fine details concerning guns
come from other sources, listed in Appendix C.

REASONS FOR ARIZONA'S GUN LAWS

Arizona criminal law begins with a list of reasons for its
existence, all of which have direct impact on gun
ownership and use:

1 - To prohibit conduct which might harm people;
2 - To give fair warning of conduct which is against the
    law and the penalties involved;
3 - To define the acts which are crimes and to limit
    condemnation of behavior which isn't criminal;
4 - To organize crimes by how bad they are, and to
    match the penalty to the crime;
5 - To discourage crime by authorizing punishment;
6 - To mete out punishment.

WHAT IS A FIREARM?

In Arizona, a firearm is defined as a *deadly weapon*, a term which includes anything designed for lethal use. Specifically, state law says that "firearm" means:

"...any loaded or unloaded pistol, revolver, rifle, shotgun or other weapon which will or is designed to or may readily be converted to expel a projectile by the action of expanding gases..."

An exception is made for a firearm which is permanently inoperable. This applies primarily to antique or collectible guns which have been thoroughly disabled and are only for show. Questions about how to make a specific gun unserviceable can be directed to the Firearms Technology Branch of the Bureau of Alcohol, Tobacco and Firearms.

All other antique, replica, curio, relic and similar firearms capable of firing (or which can be modified to fire) are treated as ordinary guns under state law.

A B•B, pellet or dart gun (using compressed air or CO_2 gas to propel the projectile) fits the main definition of a firearm. B•B guns are sometimes treated as regular firearms by the authorities, and are specifically mentioned in a few regulations. However, when describing criminal misconduct with a firearm, the law uses a special definition for guns, in which the projectile is expelled by "the action of an explosive." This clearly excludes a B•B gun's operation, but when in doubt, the safest course of action is to treat B•B guns as if they are regular firearms.

In this book, the words *gun*, *firearm* and *arms* are used interchangeably, and include handguns such as pistols and revolvers, and long guns such as rifles and shotguns.

WHAT DOES IT ALL MEAN?

Law books don't use the word *crime* — they use the terms *felony*, *misdemeanor* and *petty offense*. Crimes are divided into these categories to help match the punishment to the crime. Felonies are extremely serious, misdemeanors are serious and petty offenses can be serious.

Felonies and misdemeanors are also grouped into "classes". *Class 1* means the worst crime. Felonies go from class 1 to class 6, and misdemeanors run from class 1 to class 3. Petty offenses have no class.

See the Crime and Punishment Chart on the inside back cover for the basic penalties for each type of crime.

WHO CAN BEAR ARMS IN ARIZONA?

If you are a resident of Arizona you may have a gun unless:

1 - You have been found to be dangerous to yourself or other people by a court of law;

2 - You have been convicted of a felony involving violence or possession and use of a deadly weapon or dangerous instrument, and your civil rights have not been restored;

3 - You are serving a term of imprisonment in any correctional or detention facility.

Arizona law calls these people *prohibited possessors.* Selling or transferring a deadly weapon or ammunition to a prohibited possessor is a class 6 felony. Having a deadly weapon or ammunition if you are a prohibited possessor is a class 6 felony.

In addition, you may also be prohibited from firearm possession under federal laws designed to keep weapons out of the hands of criminals. These overriding restrictions are listed in Section 8 of the Firearm Transaction Record which must be completed when you buy a gun from a federally licensed dealer. Federal law prohibits gun purchase or possession by anyone who:

- Is charged with or has been convicted of a crime which carries more than a one-year sentence;
- Is a fugitive from justice;
- Unlawfully uses or is addicted to marijuana, a depressant, a stimulant or a narcotic drug;
- Is mentally defective;
- Is mentally incompetent;
- Is committed to a mental institution;
- Has been dishonorably discharged from the armed forces;
- Has renounced U.S. citizenship;
- Is an illegal alien.

When filling out a Firearm Transaction Record form, you are required to state that you are not in any of these categories. It is a felony to make false statements on a Firearms Transaction Record form.

There is no legal minimum age at which a child can have or use a gun. This is a choice to be made by parents or legal guardians of the minor, who have a legal obligation to act in a responsible manner. However, giving or selling a gun to a minor, without *written* consent from the minor's parent or legal guardian, is a class 2 misdemeanor.

Keep in mind that the right to bear firearms isn't the right to bear anything, anywhere, at any time. Nor is it the right to organize a body of armed individuals.

HOW DO YOU OBTAIN FIREARMS?

Guns and ammunition may be bought or sold between private individuals of this state under the same conditions as any other private sale of merchandise. If you are going to deal in guns, however, you need a license from the Bureau of Alcohol, Tobacco and Firearms. Federally licensed dealers of firearms and ammunition are spread across the state. Residents need no special license or permit to walk in and buy a regular firearm from a regular dealer. Firearms may be paid for in the same ways as any other retail merchandise.

Neither individual firearms nor firearm sales are reported or centrally registered, providing a measure of privacy for owners. There is no waiting period to receive firearms bought from a dealer's stock. There are no restrictions on the number of firearms or the amount of ammunition you may own. You may sell a gun you own to any dealer in the state.

To purchase a rifle or shotgun and matching ammunition you must be at least 18 years old. To purchase a handgun and matching ammunition you must be at least 21 years old. Some ammunition may be used in either a handgun or a rifle. This type of ammo can only be sold to a person between the ages of 18 and 21 if the dealer is satisfied that it will be used only in a rifle.

In-State Purchase

Personal identification which establishes your name, place of residence, age and your signature must be shown to the dealer. A driver's license (or a state ID card issued in place of a driver's license) is the usual form of ID expected by most dealers.

When you buy firearms you must fill out a federal Firearms Transaction Record. There are no duplicate copies made of this form, and the original is permanently filed by the dealer. The form requires personal identification information, identification of the gun and its serial number, and your signature, stating that you are not ineligible to obtain firearms under federal law. Licensed dealers keep copies of this form available.

The purchase of more than one handgun from the same dealer in a five-day period *is* reported to the Bureau of Alcohol, Tobacco and Firearms. This report must be made by the dealer before the close of business on the day of the sale.

Out-of-State Purchases

Residents of this state, including businesses and corporations, are specifically granted permission in the statutes to buy guns anywhere in the United States. Such purchases must conform to the local laws at the place of purchase. However, the overlapping local, state and federal gun laws in the U.S. are frequently incompatible, and can sometimes make this difficult.

When you buy a long gun out of state, you may take delivery immediately. Federal law requires that handguns purchased out of state must be shipped to you via a licensed dealer in your home state - you cannot take possession of the gun over the counter.

WHAT DO YOU NEED TO GET A FIREARM?

WHAT DO YOU NEED TO GET A FIREARM?

- You must be over 18 years old for a long gun, over 21 for a hand gun.
- You must have identification which establishes your name, residence, date of birth, and your signature.
- You must be a law-abiding citizen with no serious criminal record.
- If you are not a resident of Arizona, it must be legal for you to have the weapon in your home state.
- You must have enough money or credit to make the purchase.

Gun Shows

Gun shows are periodically sponsored by national, state and local organizations devoted to the collection, competitive use or other sporting use of firearms. You may purchase firearms from an in-state dealer at a gun show the same as you could on their regular retail premises. Out-of-state dealers can display their wares and take orders, but cannot make deliveries at the show. Purchases made from an out-of-state dealer must be shipped to a licensee within this state, from the out-of-state dealer's licensed premises.

CARRYING FIREARMS

You may carry firearms, loaded or unloaded, throughout the state of Arizona, subject to the restrictions which follow. If you carry a gun on yourself it must be at least partially visible or in a belt holster which is at least partially visible. A gun may also be carried in a scabbard or case designed for carrying weapons. The scabbard or case must be at least partially visible, or else carried in luggage.

Guns in Cars

You can carry a gun, loaded or unloaded, anywhere in a car (or other means of transportation) if it is in a case, holster, scabbard, pack, luggage or if it is plainly visible. It may also be kept in a storage compartment, trunk or the glove compartment of the vehicle.

Concealed Weapons

In Arizona it's generally against the law to carry a gun concealed on yourself. Carrying a concealed weapon is a class 1 misdemeanor.

There are only three places where you may legally carry a concealed gun on yourself in this state:

1 - In your own dwelling;
2 - On your business premises;
3 - On real estate owned or leased by you.

It's illegal to have an unholstered gun concealed and within immediate control of any person in a car or other means of transportation. Violation is a class 1 misdemeanor.

Local, state and federal authorities may be permitted to carry concealed weapons. No such permits exist for regular citizens of Arizona.

Prohibited Places

- You cannot enter any public establishment or attend any public event and carry a gun after the people in charge of the establishment or event ask you to give them the gun. Failure to leave or place the gun in their custody is a class 1 misdemeanor. A sign prohibiting guns at an entrance point is a sufficient request to leave your gun outside.

- Going into a polling place with a gun, on the day of an election, is a class 1 misdemeanor.

- Except for limited hunting privileges, there is a fine of up to $500 for carrying a gun in the National Parks.

- Possession of firearms on a military base is subject to control by the commanding officer.

- On a game refuge, possession of a loaded gun for taking game, without special written permission from the Arizona Game and Fish Commission, is a class 2 misdemeanor.

- It's a class 2 felony to bring a gun into a correctional facility or its grounds.

- It's a class 5 felony to bring a gun into or around a juvenile correction facility.

- It's a class 1 misdemeanor to have a firearm on school grounds. See chapter 4 for exceptions.

- You can't have a gun in a federal facility, except while hunting or for other legal reason. You cannot be convicted of this violation unless notices are posted.

WHEN CAN YOU CONCEAL A FIREARM?

WHEN CAN YOU CONCEAL A FIREARM?

The question isn't *when*, it's *where*. The three *places* where you may conceal a gun on yourself are:

1 - In your residence;
2 - On your business premises;
3 - On land owned or leased by you.

For private citizens, there are no other "times" allowed under the law.

Confusion occasionally arises since, in some cases, a gun may be concealed from sight without being a violation of the concealed weapons laws. Two common examples would include a gun in a gun case and a gun in a glovebox.

Bars

It's generally illegal to have a firearm in a place which is licensed to serve alcohol. If you walk in and don't know it's illegal you're excused once. (The law says it's illegal to walk in with a firearm "knowing such possession is prohibited"). Having a gun in a bar is a class 2 misdemeanor.

It's illegal for the licensee of a bar to allow a person with a firearm to remain on the premises. It's illegal for the licensee to supply you with liquor knowing you're armed. These are both class 2 misdemeanors. A licensee must call the police to remove an armed person, if necessary. The State Liquor Board can suspend, revoke, or refuse to renew a liquor license for failure to comply.

The law allows a few exceptions:

1 - Hotel and motel guest accomodations are excluded.

2 - The licensee of a bar, and employees who the licensee authorizes, may carry firearms.

3 - A liquor-licensed establishment can have an exhibition or display of firearms in connection with a meeting, show, class or similar event.

4 - If you enter a bar to seek emergency aid, and you receive no alcohol, you may legally carry firearms.

TYPES OF WEAPONS 2

There are weapons and there are weapons. A gun may be perfectly legal, but if you wear it under your jacket, it becomes a *concealed weapon*... and that is usually a crime. If a gun has been modified in certain ways, it becomes a *prohibited weapon* and it may be a crime to possess it at all.

Weapons include *dangerous instruments*, things which can be deadly depending on their use, like fireplace tools or a baseball bat. *Deadly weapons* specifically refers to things which are designed for lethal use. Guns are only one kind of deadly weapon.

PROHIBITED WEAPONS

In 1934, responding to mob violence spawned by Prohibition, Congress passed the National Firearms Act (NFA), the first federal law concerning guns since the Constitution. This was an attempt to control what Congress called "gangster-type weapons". Items like machine guns, silencers, short rifles and sawed-off shotguns were put under strict government control and registration. These became known as "NFA weapons."

This gave authorities a legal weapon in the fight against crime. Criminals never registered their weapons, and now simple possession of an unregistered "gangster gun" was a federal offense. Failure to have paid the required transfer tax on the weapon compounded the charge. Regular types of personal firearms were completely unaffected.

Political assassinations in the 1960's led to a public outcry for greater gun controls. In 1968 the federal Gun Control Act was passed, which absorbed the provisions of earlier statutes, and added bombs and other destructive devices to the list of strictly controlled weapons. Arizona calls these *prohibited weapons*, though a more accurate title might be *controlled weapons*, as you'll see under Machine Guns. It is generally illegal to make, have, transport, sell or transfer any prohibited weapon without prior approval and registration. Violation of this is a class 4 felony under state law, and carries federal penalties of up to 10 years in jail and up to a $10,000 fine.

ILLEGAL GUNS
(Also called NFA weapons or prohibited weapons)

These weapons and destructive devices are illegal unless they are pre-registered with the Bureau of Alcohol, Tobacco and Firearms.

1 - A rifle with a barrel less than 16 inches long
2 - A shotgun with a barrel less than 18 inches long
3 - A modified rifle or shotgun less than 26 inches overall
4 - Machine guns
5 - Silencers of any kind
6 - Firearms over .50 caliber

Guns with a bore of greater than one-half inch are technically known as destructive devices. Some antique and black powder firearms have such large bores but are not prohibited, as determined on a case by case basis by the Bureau of Alcohol, Tobacco and Firearms.

A number of other deadly weapons which are not guns are also prohibited under state and federal law:

OTHER ILLEGAL DEADLY WEAPONS

(Also called destructive devices)

1 - Explosive, incendiary or poison gas bombs
2 - Explosive, incendiary or poison gas grenades
3 - Explosive, incendiary or poison gas rockets with more than 4 ounces of propellant (includes bazooka)
4 - Explosive, incendiary or poison gas mines
5 - Mortars
6 - Nunchaku (a martial arts weapon made of two sticks, clubs, bars or rods, connected by a rope, cord, wire or chain. Nunchaku are not prohibited in lawful martial arts pursuits.)
7 - Armor piercing ammunition (a handgun bullet with at least a core of steel, iron, brass, bronze, beryllium copper, depleted uranium or one or a combination of tungsten alloys. Excluded are nontoxic shotgun shot, frangible projectiles designed for target shooting, projectiles intended for industrial purposes, oil and gas well perforating devices, and ammunition which is intended for sporting purposes.)
8 - Missiles with an explosive or incendiary charge greater than 1/4 ounce.

Defaced Deadly Weapons

Removing, altering or destroying the manufacturer's serial number on a gun is a class 6 felony. Knowingly having a defaced gun is a class 6 felony.

MACHINE GUNS

Under strictly regulated conditions, private citizens can have weapons which would otherwise be prohibited. An example is the machine gun.

Unlike normal firearm possession, the cloak of privacy afforded gun ownership is removed in the case of so-called "NFA weapons" - those which were originally restricted by the National Firearms Act of 1934. The list has grown since that time, through subsequent legislation. For a law-abiding private citizen to have an NFA weapon, five conditions must be met. These requirements are designed to keep the weapons out of criminal hands, or to prosecute criminals for possession.

1 - The weapon itself must be registered in the National Firearms Registry and Transfer Records of the Treasury Department. This list of arms includes about 193,000 machine guns.

2 - Permission to transfer the weapon must be obtained in advance, by filing "ATF Form 4 (5320.4)" available from the Bureau of Alcohol, Tobacco and Firearms.

3 - An FBI check of your background is performed to locate any criminal record which would disqualify you from possessing the weapon. This is done with the help of a recent 2" x 2" photograph of yourself and your fingerprints on an FBI form FD-258 Fingerprint Card, which must be submitted with the application.

4 - The transfer of the weapon from its lawful owner to you must be federally registered. In other words, a central record is kept of every NFA weapon and its current owner.

5 - You must pay a $200 transfer tax. For some NFA weapons, the transfer tax is $5.00.

A properly licensed dealer can sell a registered machine gun to a qualified private buyer.

You may apply for approval to make NFA weapons, such as short rifles or sawed-off shotguns. The application process is similar to the process for buying such weapons. Unregistered NFA weapons are contraband, and are subject to seizure. Having the unassembled parts needed to make an NFA weapon counts as having one.

The authorities are generally exempt from these provisions. Open trade in automatic weapons in Arizona is allowed between manufacturers and dealers, and includes state and city police, prisons, the state and federal military, museums, educational institutions, and people with special licenses and permits.

The official trade in machine guns is specifically prohibited from becoming a source of commercial supply. Only those machine guns (and other NFA weapons) which were in the National Firearms Registry and Transfer Records as of May 19, 1986 may be privately held. This includes about 6,600 machine guns in Arizona. The number available nationally will likely drop, since no new full-autos are being added to the registry, and the existing supply will decrease through attrition. Arizona has about 18,000 NFA weapons in total.

CURIOS AND RELICS

Curios and Relics are guns which have special value as antiquities, for historical purposes, or other reasons which make it unlikely that they will be used currently as weapons. The Curio and Relic List is a 60-page document available from the Bureau of Alcohol, Tobacco and Firearms. They can also tell you how to apply to obtain curio or relic status for a particular weapon.

HOW CAN YOU CARRY A GUN?

HOW CAN YOU CARRY A GUN?

The main point to consider is that, in Arizona, a gun cannot be carried *concealed on yourself* in public. The top two pictures show illegal ways to carry.

The law says it's not illegal to carry weapons:

> "...in a belt holster which holster is wholly or partially visible,"

or:

> "...in a scabbard or case designed for carrying weapons which scabbard or case is wholly or partially visible or carried in luggage."

Although the law *allows* weapons to be carried in a belt holster, it doesn't *require* that they be carried that way.

In a car or other means of transportation, you cannot conceal an unholstered gun within the immediate control of any person. You can have a gun in a car if it is in a case, holster or scabbard, or if it is in a storage compartment, trunk, pack, luggage or glove compartment, or if it is in plain sight.

WHERE CAN YOU SHOOT? 3

Once you own a gun, it's natural to want to go out and fire it. If you've decided to keep a gun, you should learn how it works and be able to handle it with confidence. Public ranges provide an excellent and safe opportunity. Many people also enjoy shooting outdoors on open terrain.

The 72.5 million acres of Arizona are regulated by many different authorities. The Bureau of Land Management (BLM) has a map available called the *Surface Management Responsibility* map, which gives an excellent overview of what's what. The map has certain limitations, not the least of which is its issue date, 1979, but it is a valuable reference nonetheless. Exact up-to-date records are kept by BLM, and an updated map is expected out in the future.

In order to understand where you can shoot outdoors in this state, you must first know where you cannot shoot. The restrictions come first when determining if shooting in an area is permissible.

Certain legal justifications may allow shooting, even if it would otherwise be illegal. An example is self-defense. A list of justifications is in Chapter 4.

GENERAL RESTRICTIONS

Illegal Trajectory

It is illegal to shoot if the bullet will travel anywhere where it may create a hazard to life or property. In National Forests, you may not shoot from or across a body of water adjacent to a road.

Aside from being a violation of several laws, there is a general rule of gun safety here: Be sure of your backstop. Take this a step further: Be sure of your line of fire. Never fire if you are unaware of (or not in full control of) the complete possible trajectory of the bullet. Be sure that the shot poses no threat to life or property.

The Quarter-Mile Rule

Shooting while hunting is prohibited within one-quarter mile of any residence or building that could serve as a residence whether occupied or not, or any other developed facility of any kind. A car or other vehicle (other than your own) counts as an object which you must be at least a quarter of a mile away from when you discharge your firearm.

Although this rule comes from and applies specifically to hunting regulations, authorities use the quarter-mile rule as a guideline for determining if gun use is safe. Don't take chances. Make sure you are at *least* a quarter of a mile from *anything* when you are shooting.

From Vehicles

It's illegal to fire a gun (without a handicap permit) from a vehicle while hunting. This includes an automobile, pickup, off-road vehicle, motorcycle, aircraft, train, powerboat, sailboat, floating object towed by a sailboat or powerboat or any device designed to carry a person. (Requirements for hunting waterfowl are different.) It's also illegal to knowingly shoot upon, from, across or into a road or railway while hunting, or while in the National Forests.

Once again, hunting regulations provide restrictions which aren't specifically regulated in most other state statutes. However, authorities frown on "road shooting," and it is extremely unsafe. Shooting from vehicles or on or around roads is not a good idea.

Posted Areas

Signs can be posted which restrict firearm use, possession, or access to land or premises.

- *Private Land* may be posted by authority of the landowner or lessee.

- *State Land* may be posted by the lessee, but only with permission from the Commissioner of the Arizona State Land Department.

- *National Forests* may have areas posted for a number of reasons by the authorities.

- *The Arizona Game and Fish Department* can post an area to restrict hunting.

Even *a store*, or any other *public place* or *public event* can post a sign restricting firearm possession. Most private, local, tribal, state and federal authorities may legally post an area under their control. The penalty for a violation varies depending upon who posted what area.

THE LAND OF ARIZONA

Bureau of Land Management Land (BLM)

16% of the state's land - about 12 million acres - is managed by BLM under a doctrine of multiple use and sustained yield. What this means is that recreationists share the lands with ranchers, miners and other users. BLM land is as close as there is to truly "public land."

The Arizona state BLM office in Phoenix maintains the maps (called Master Title Plats) and the current records

WHAT'S WRONG WITH THIS PICTURE?

WHAT'S WRONG WITH THIS PICTURE?

1 - Shooting within city limits is normally prohibited.

2 - It's illegal to shoot or harm a cactus.

3 - It's illegal to deface signs.

4 - Trespassing is illegal.

5 - You can't use targets which leave debris.

6 - Shooting at wildlife requires a permit or license.

7 - The target has no backstop. The shooter is not controlling the entire trajectory of the bullet.

8 - The shooter isn't wearing eye or ear protection.

on land status for the entire state. It is an invaluable resource for determining what land is what. Two maps published by BLM are excellent general references for shooters. The *Surface Management Map* provides an overview of the whole state at a glance. The *Wilderness Status Map* shows all BLM areas under special restrictions as wilderness preserves.

Shooting on BLM land is legal as long as you comply with the normal state regulations. A few special considerations apply:

- Observe posted closures. BLM land generally isn't posted, although main entry points may have signs. Special Management Areas and other sections may have posted restrictions.

- Avoid conflicts with lessees.

- Avoid developed areas.

- The Long Term Visitor Area (LTVA) of La Posa in the Yuma district, and the land within one-half mile of the LTVA is closed to shooting and hunting.

- It's illegal to willfully deface, disturb or destroy any personal property, natural object or area, structures, or scientific, cultural, archaeological or historical resource.

- It's illegal to willfully deface or destroy plants or their parts, soil, rocks or minerals.

Hunting on BLM land is allowed, subject to the regulations of the Arizona Game and Fish Department. However, BLM authorities can close sections to shooting, or restrict or close access to public lands, when and where safety or other valid reasons may require.

Knowingly and willfully violating BLM regulations carries a maximum $1000 fine and up to one year in jail. Violators may be subject to civil damages as well. BLM district offices are listed in Appendix C.

Cities

It is usually illegal to shoot within the boundaries of any city in the state. Municipalities are a no-fire zone, and can have their own special regulations prohibiting shooting within city limits. State law makes this a class 2 misdemeanor. The exceptions are described below.

Firing Ranges - Shooting within city limits can be allowed on a properly supervised range. See "Shooting Ranges" in this chapter for a description of such ranges.

B•B Guns - Individual cities may have their own rules concerning B•B guns. It may be permissable to set up a B•B gun range indoors or outdoors within municipal boundaries if proper safety measures are taken. Check with local authorities for exact details on your location.

Designated Hunting Ranges - An area within a city may be designated a hunting area by the Arizona Game and Fish Department. If the chief of police of the city agrees and posts proper notices, then shooting is legal. This allowance can be revoked anytime the authorities decide it is unsafe.

Control of Nuisance Wildlife - A required permit is available for this purpose from the Arizona Game and Fish Department or from the United States Fish and Wildlife Service. Problems with nuisance wildlife can often be handled best by contacting an exterminator who has the proper permits.

Special Permit - The chief of police of a city may issue a special permit for firing guns within city limits.

Legally Justified Instances - The law allows shooting within city limits under certain narrow circumstances called *justification*. An example is self-defense. For details see Chapter 4.

County Land

The state of Arizona is divided into 15 counties: Apache, Cochise, Coconino, Gila, Graham, Greenlee, Lapaz,

Maricopa, Mohave, Navajo, Pima, Pinal, Santa Cruz, Yavapai and Yuma. In nine of these, the only lands generally owned by the county are small parcels which contain the sherrif's office, the county courthouse, the jail, vehicle depots or similar facilities.

In addition to administrative sites, six counties maintain a park system. The offices for the park systems of Coconino, Maricopa, Mohave, Navajo, Pima and Yavapai counties are listed in Appendix C.

County parks used to be open to firearm use, but because of increasing population and the relatively small sizes of these parks, firearm use is now extremely limited. In general, rifled firearms and target practice are prohibited in county parks. Shotgun (smooth bore) hunting on these lands is regulated by the Arizona Game and Fish Department. If and when prudent wildlife management requires, strictly controlled rifled firearm hunting may be allowed by AGFD in cooperation with the park authorities.

County land may contain authorized shooting ranges, and in fact one of the state's best equipped ranges, the Black Canyon Range, is on land leased by the Maricopa county parks.

Indian Country

Fourteen Indian tribes - better than 200,000 people - live in Arizona on 20 reservations. More than 19 million acres are included in this land, amounting to 28% of the state.

Each reservation maintains its own government, and operates almost as a separate nation. A Tribal Council, headed by a Chairman, Chairperson, President or Governor, makes laws regarding guns on Indian land. You must contact a specific reservation to get current information and valid permits for their land. No state license, permit or tags are required by the state for hunting in Indian Country. The address and telephone number for each reservation is listed in Appendix C.

Many reservations encourage hunting (and other use) of their land, with proper tribal permits and within regulations. Hunting does not necessarily mean firearms are allowed. For example, hunting is permitted by the Navajos on the largest reservation in the state, but a tribal code prohibits the use of firearms. Some tribes offer no guidelines on the subject.

Overlapping federal, state, tribal and local authority creates confusion when laws are violated in Indian Country. Enforcement of laws on Indian reservations can cause a fundamental conflict over jurisdiction. Actual penalties for violations may be the subject of dispute. The Arizona Commission on Indian Affairs calls for the federal government to take ultimate responsibility for prosecution of crimes committed on Indian lands by non-Indians.

National Forests

15% of Arizona - about 11 million acres - is made up of National Forests operated by the Forest Service of the U.S. Department of Agriculture. You may carry firearms at anytime and anywhere in the National Forests, as long as you and your gun are in compliance with the law. Don't confuse the National Forests with the National Parks (listed later), where you normally may not even carry a loaded gun.

Hunting is allowed in the National Forests, but requires proper licenses. Contact the Arizona Game and Fish Department for details. Also see the separate section on "Hunting Regulations" in Chapter 4.

Target shooters are required to use removable targets. Clay pigeons, bottles, trash and other targets which leave debris are prohibited. Your choice of a target site should be against an embankment which will prevent bullets from causing a hazard. Your location should be *remote* from populated sites.

The laws controlling the National Forests are in a book called *Code of Federal Regulations, Title 36*, available at larger libraries. These federal rules prohibit shooting:

- Within 150 yards of a residence, building, campsite, developed recreation site or occupied area;
- Across or on a Forest Development road;
- Across or on a body of water adjacent to a Forest Development road;
- In any way which puts people at risk of injury or puts property at risk of damage;
- Which kills or injures any timber, tree or forest product;
- Which makes unreasonable noise;
- Which damages any natural feature or property of the United States.

Violation of these restrictions carries a possible $500 fine and a maximum prison sentence of 6 months under federal law.

The Forest Supervisor or other proper authority may issue special restrictions on firearm possession or use, or close a section to access if it seems necessary to protect public safety, or for other good reason.

For example, a small section of Tonto National Forest known as the "Lower Salt River Recreation Area" has been closed to guns and B•B guns, *except* for licensed hunting, since October 1985, for safety reasons. The Superstition Wilderness within Tonto National Forest has had a similar restriction in effect since February 1985. In the Sabino Canyon Recreation Area you may not even *have* firearms, except for hunters passing through to the hunt area. It's always wise to check with a representative of the Forest Service about any piece of National Forest land you're planning on using. National Forests and their offices in the state of Arizona are listed in Appendix C.

National Parks Service Land

The National Parks Service of the U.S. Department of the Interior manages 22 national sites in Arizona, more than any other state. This includes National Parks, National Monuments, National Historic Sites and National Recreation Areas.

Limited hunting privileges exist in National Recreation Areas by special agreement of the Department of the Interior and the Arizona Game and Fish Department. Except for this, it's illegal to even carry a loaded firearm into the National Parks Service lands. Firearms must be unloaded, cased and out of sight, and broken down (bolt or magazine removed or otherwise temporarily inoperable). A list of Arizona's National Parks Service sites is in Appendix C.

Private Land

You can shoot on your own land as long as you don't violate any regulations. That means you need enough land to shoot safely, at least a quarter-mile from any roads, outside of municipal boundaries, without disturbing the peace, and so forth. 18% of Arizona - approximately 13 million acres - is owned privately or by corporations.

Land owners may grant permission for others to shoot on their land and may allow access to the public. Permission can be withdrawn at will. To prohibit shooting on private land, the landowner or lessee must put up plainly legible signs, at least eight by eleven inches in size, no more than a quarter-mile apart, around the entire protected area.

Shooting Ranges

Officially approved shooting ranges may be the best place to learn and practice the shooting sports. Ranges may be legally set up within city limits as long as they are operated by:

- A club affiliated with the National Rifle Association, The Amateur Trapshooting Association, The National Skeet Association, or any other nationally recognized shooting organization;
- Any agency of the federal government;

WHERE ARE GUNS FORBIDDEN?

- Any public establishment and any public event in the state can prohibit weapons at the site. They can post signs or ask you to remove your weapons. If there aren't facilities for checking weapons (and there usually aren't since there are substantial liabilities in checking weapons), you had best leave your guns outside.

- You can't bring a gun into a polling place on the day of an election.

- You can't carry a gun (except for licensed hunting) in the National Parks.

- You can't carry weapons on a military base without permission from the commanding officer.

- You can't have a loaded gun for taking game on a game refuge without written permission from the Arizona Game and Fish Commission.

- You can't bring a gun onto or around the grounds of a juvenile correctional facility, or into a prison or its grounds.

- You can't bring a gun into a place licensed to serve alcohol except for:
  — The boss, who can also authorize employees
  — Hotel or motel accommodations
  — Gun shows and similar events
  — In an emergency to seek aid, provided you get no alcohol.

- You can't have a gun in a federal facility, except while hunting or for other legal reason. You cannot be convicted of this violation unless notices are posted.

- You can't have a firearm on school grounds except for hunter or firearm safety courses, or for an authorized school program. Exceptions for vehicles and transporting pupils are covered in Chapter 4.

- An agency of state, county or city government which will have the range within its boundaries;
- Public or private schools.

For underground ranges on private or public property, only adult supervision is required. B•B guns may be used on a range operated with adult supervision.

State and Federal Military Land

Land reserved for military use, whether under the jurisdiction of the National Guard or a branch of the federal armed forces such as the Army or the Air Force, is controlled by a military commander. What a commander says, goes. Possession or use of firearms on a military base is subject to control by the commanding officer.

You can't do much of anything on military land without prior approval. In general, military shooting ranges are not available for public use. Where limited hunting privileges are available, they are subject to the regulations of the Arizona Game and Fish Department *and* the base commander. Anyone on military land is subject to a search. For details concerning a specific military installation, contact the base provost marshall or the base commander's office.

Carrying firearms while traveling on a public road which passes through military land is subject to standard state regulations.

State Land

13% of Arizona is managed by the Arizona State Land Department, and leased out under guidelines which require productive use of the land. You must have a permit to be on the nearly 10 million acres of state land. Trespassing is a class 2 misdemeanor.

State land, even though it may be under lease for grazing, agriculture, or any other purpose, is usually open to licensed hunting and fishing. Wildlife on state land belongs to the state, and so it is regulated by the Arizona Game and Fish Department.

A person with valid licenses and tags, engaging in a lawful hunt, is allowed on state land. In effect, a hunting license is a written exemption from the "No Trespassing - State Land" signs. Other people using the land, or hunters engaging in any other activites besides those normally involved in a lawful hunt, would be trespassing unless they had received special authorization.

Recreation permits are available for camping and other non-consumptive use of state land, but use of firearms is not included in these specially issued permits.

While you are on state land, it's illegal to intentionally or wantonly destroy, deface, injure, remove or disturb anything made and put there by people, or to harm or take away any natural feature, object of natural beauty, antiquity or other public or private property. A violation is a class 2 misdemeanor.

State Parks

Arizona has 25 state parks on about 45,000 acres of land. These are managed by Arizona State Parks. Hunting in the state parks is regulated by the Arizona Game and Fish Department.

Because of the relatively small size of these parks and the large number of people using them, use of firearms except for licensed hunting is discouraged. Shooting is illegal in and around developed areas of any kind. Firearms may be carried in the parks, but in park buildings or developed recreation areas, Park Rangers may request that you remove your weapons. Upon a reasonable request, you must either place the weapon in the Ranger's custody or leave the building or area.

RELATED LAWS 4

**"I got my questionnaire baby,
You know I'm headed off for war,
Well now I'm gonna kill somebody,
Don't have to break no kind of law."**

- from a traditional blues song

There are times when you may shoot and kill another person and be guilty of no crime under Arizona law. The law calls this *justification*. Justification is a complete defense against any criminal or civil charges. The specific circumstances of a shooting determine whether the shooting is justified, and if not, which crime has been committed. Justification in killing someone does not provide criminal or civil protection for recklessly killing an innocent third person in the process.

Whenever a shooting occurs, a crime has been committed. Either the shooting is legal as a defense against a crime or attempted crime, or else the shooting is not justified, in which case the shooting itself is the crime.

USE OF DEADLY PHYSICAL FORCE

A reasonable person hopes that it will never be necessary to raise a weapon in self-defense. It's smart to always avoid such confrontations. In the unlikely event that you must resort to force to defend yourself, you are generally required to use as little force as necessary to control your situation. Your own life is permanently changed if you ever kill another human being, intentionally or otherwise.

No matter how well you understand the law, or how justified you feel you may be in a shooting incident, your fate will probably be determined much later, in a court of law. Establishing the facts precisely can be an impossible task. What were the exact circumstances, as you remember them? Were there witnesses, who are they, and what will they remember and say to the authorities and in a courtroom? What was your relationship to the deceased person? Has there been even a single case recently which affects how the law is now interpreted? Was a new law put into place yesterday? How good is your lawyer? How convincing are you? What will the jury think?

You could be on much safer ground if you use a gun to protect yourself *without* actually firing a shot. The number of crimes which are prevented by the presence of a citizen's gun *which isn't fired* are estimated to be in the hundreds of thousands. Be smart and never shoot at anyone if there is any way at all to avoid it.

Still, the law recognizes your right to protect yourself, your loved ones, and other people from certain criminal acts. You are urged to read the actual language of the law about this critical subject, and even then, to avoid taking human life if at all possible.

Even with a good understanding of the rules, there may be more to it than meets the eye. As just one example, shooting a criminal who is fleeing a crime is treated differently by the law than shooting a criminal who is in the act of committing a crime. The law is strict, complex and not something to take chances with in the heat of the moment if you don't have to.

It's natural to want to know, beforehand, just when it's OK to shoot to kill and be able to claim self-defense. Unfortunately, you'll never know for sure until *after* a situation arises. You make your moves whatever they are, and the authorities or a jury decides. The law doesn't physically control what you can or can't *do* - it gives the authorities guidelines on how to evaluate what you did after it occurs. There are legal risks when you choose to use force.

The "§" (Section) symbol used below refers to the related section of the Arizona Revised Statutes, which can be found in Appendix D.

"The quotations below are plain, conversational expressions of the gist of the law." This is followed by a more precise description of the law. Finally, each subject is cross-referenced to the actual section ("§") of the law.

Maintaining Order

"The person in charge can keep the peace."

If you are responsible for keeping order in a place where people are gathered you are justified in using deadly physical force if it is reasonably necessary to prevent death or serious physical injury. A person responsible for keeping order on a common motor carrier of passengers also has this justification. See §13-403 for the letter of the law.

Self-Defense

"Only when someone is about to kill you can you kill them first."

You are justified in threatening or using deadly physical force against another person to protect your life, only if a reasonable person would believe that your life is immediately and illegally threatened by the other person. If your life is being threatened by someone because of

CONTINUED ON PAGE 58

IF YOU SHOOT A CROOK OUTSIDE YOUR HOUSE
DO YOU HAVE TO DRAG HIM INSIDE?

IF YOU SHOOT A CROOK OUTSIDE YOUR HOUSE DO YOU HAVE TO DRAG HIM INSIDE?

No! Acting on this wide-spread myth is a completely terrible idea. You're talking about tampering with evidence, obstructing justice, interfering with official procedures and more. If you're involved in a shooting, leave everything at the scene just as it is and call for the police and an ambulance.

Don't think for a minute that modern forensics won't detect an altered scene of a crime. At any shooting a crime has been committed. Either the shooting is justified, which means you were in your rights and the victim was acting illegally, or you exceeded your rights in the shooting, regardless of the victim's circumstance. The situation will be investigated to determine the facts, and believe it, the facts will come out. Police tell time-worn jokes about finding "black heel marks on the linoleum." And once you're caught in a lie, your credibility is shot.

If you tamper with the evidence, you have to lie to all the authorities to back it up. Then you have to commit perjury to follow through. Can you pull it off?

If the guy with the mask was shot from the front, armed as he is, the homeowner has a good case for self-defense. If the masked man was shot from behind, the homeowner has a case for acting to prevent 1st degree burglary. Either way, he's better off leaving the body where it falls.

Suppose you shoot an armed intruder coming through your window, and the body falls outside the house. You'll have a better time convincing a jury that you were scared to death, than trying to explain how the dead crook in your living room got blood stains on your lawn.

The reason this fable gets so much play is because there is a big difference between a homeowner shooting a crook in the kitchen, and one person shooting another outdoors. Shooting at a stranger outside your house can be murder.

criminal activities you are doing, self-defense is probably not a valid claim. See §13-404 and §13-405 for the letter of the law.

The law says that if you provoke another person to attempt to use deadly force on you, you may lose your justification. However, it also says that if you provoke someone, then back down and they don't back down, you may be justified. You are never justified in response to verbal provocation alone. See §13-404 for the letter of the law.

Defense of a Third Person

"You can protect someone else the same as you can protect yourself."

You are justified in threatening or using deadly physical force to protect a third person under the same circumstances as you would to protect yourself: if a reasonable person would believe that your actions are immediately necessary to protect the third person against the use of unlawful deadly physical force. See §13-406 for the letter of the law.

Defense of Premises

"You can't kill to protect your property, but you can threaten to protect it."

You or someone acting for you is justified in threatening to use deadly physical force in order to stop someone from criminally trespassing on your land or premises. Using deadly physical force is *not* justified unless you are actually defending your life, the life of a third person, or if one of the crimes listed under "Crime Prevention" (see below) is being committed. See §13-407 for the letter of the law.

Law Enforcement

"You can shoot to control certain criminal activities related to arrest and escape."

NOTE: On September 15, 1989, this section of the law was changed to prohibit a private citizen from shooting at a fleeing suspect. The language used to make the change unexpectedly altered other parts of this law, which basically describes your rights and limits for firearms use in law enforcement situations. For example, the new law now conflicts with the self-defense laws. Under certain circumstances it says if you are being shot at, you can only threaten to shoot back. Although some experts agree that this is an unintentional error needing correction, other experts feel it is acceptable as is. It is the law until changed by the state legislature, and its effects on an actual case are uncertain. See §13-410 for the letter of the law.

Crime Prevention

"You can shoot to prevent certain crimes."

You are justified in using deadly physical force if you reasonably believe it is immediately necessary to prevent someone from committing:

1 - Arson of an occupied structure (§13-1704)
2 - First or second degree burglary (§13-1507, 8)
3 - Kidnapping (§13-1304)
4 - Manslaughter (§13-1103)
5 - First or second degree murder (§13-1104, 5)
6 - Sexual conduct with a minor (§13-1405)
7 - Sexual assault (§13-1406)
8 - Child molestation (§13-1410)
9 - Armed robbery (§13-1904)
10 - Aggravated assault (§13-1204, A, 1 & 2)

The law does not require you to retreat before threatening to use or using deadly physical force under the circumstances listed above. See §13-411 for the letter of the law.

OTHER LAWS

Aggravated Assault

"You can't shoot or threaten to shoot someone without a legal reason."

Intentionally, knowingly or recklessly shooting a person (or causing serious bodily injury in any other way, for that matter) without legal justification, is aggravated assault, a class 3 felony. Threatening to shoot someone is also aggravated assault. See §13-1204 for the letter of the law.

Endangerment

"You can't just point a gun at someone."

It's against the law to recklessly put another person at substantial risk of imminent death or physical injury. When a risk of death is involved, endangerment is a class 6 felony. In all other cases, endangerment is a class 1 misdemeanor. See §13-1201 for the letter of the law.

Threatening or Intimidating

"You can't threaten a person with a gun."

Attempting to terrify anyone by threatening or intimidating them with physical injury or serious damage to their property is a class 1 misdemeanor. See §13-1202 for the letter of the law.

Disorderly Conduct

"You must act seriously with guns."

It's illegal to recklessly handle, display or shoot a gun with the intention of disturbing the peace and quiet of a neighborhood, family or person. It's illegal to make unreasonable noise. Either of these violations is a class 1 misdemeanor. See §13-2904 for the letter of the law.

Hindering Prosecution

"It's illegal to help someone evade the law."

Providing a person with a gun to help them avoid a felony, is a class 5 felony. Providing a gun to someone to help them avoid a misdemeanor or petty offense, is a class 1 misdemeanor. See §13-2510 to §13-2512 for the letter of the law.

Criminal Nuisance

"It's illegal to endanger other people."

Recklessly creating or maintaining a condition which endangers the safety or health of others is a class 3 misdemeanor. See §13-2908 for the letter of the law.

Reporting Gunshot Wounds

"It's a crime to treat a gunshot wound and not report it."

A physician, surgeon, nurse or hospital attendant who is called on to treat a gunshot wound which may have resulted from illegal activity must immediately notify the authorities, and report the circumstances. Failure to make a report is a class 3 misdemeanor.

Surrender of Weapons

"Any public place or event can prohibit guns."

You are required to surrender any deadly weapons in your possession if you are at a public establishment or event, and you are asked to do so by the people in charge. Failure to leave or turn over your weapons is a class 1 misdemeanor. See §13-3102 for the letter of the law.

Peace officers, members of the military, or other persons specifically licensed or authorized, in the performance of official duties, may be excluded from surrendering their weapons.

Forfeiture of Weapons

"The authorities can take your weapons if they have just cause."

Firearms may be seized by a peace officer during an arrest or search, or if the officer has probable cause to believe that there is a threat to safety or health, or that the firearms are subject to seizure. See §13-4305 for the letter of the law. If you have, use or display a firearm in violation of any public school rule, the firearm must be forfeited. See §13-2911 for the letter of the law.

CONTINUED ON PAGE 63

CAN YOU POINT A GUN AT SOMEONE?

CAN YOU POINT A GUN AT SOMEONE?

No matter how many aces a person is holding, you can't settle the matter with a gun. This also shows how the law can be interpreted in more than one way.

If the gun you draw is loaded, you create a substantial risk of imminent death, a class 6 felony called *endangerment*. (Without the risk of death endangerment is a class 1 misdemeanor.) Using a gun to put a person in reasonable fear of imminent physical injury is *aggravated assault* - a class 3 felony. A more lenient view would be to say that this is "reckless display of a gun," which is *disorderly conduct*, a class 1 misdemeanor. Merely flashing a gun can be *threatening or intimidating*, which is a class 1 misdemeanor.

When you go to court, it could be argued that this is actually *attempted murder*. And if the guy with the gun is angry enough to take back his money, it becomes *armed robbery*.

By drawing your gun, the other guy may be able to shoot you dead and legally claim self-defense.

Despite all this, the law recognizes your right to defend yourself, your loved ones, and other people. The law also recognizes a citizen's right to act to prevent certain crimes. These cases, when you *can* point a gun at another person, are described in Chapter 4.

CONTINUED FROM PAGE 61

School Grounds

Having a firearm on school grounds in a class 1 misde- meanor, unless:

- It is directly related to hunter or firearm safety courses; or
- It is for use on the school grounds in a program approved by a school; or
- It is unloaded and in a locked container within a means of transportation which is not under the control of a pupil; or
- It is in a means of transportation when a pupil is being taken to or from school grounds, by a person other than the pupil, authorized to transport the pupil.

A school is a public or nonpublic kindergarten program, common school, or high school. See §13-3102 for the letter of the law.

If you are convicted of a felony involving one or more guns, you forfeit the weapons. The state either keeps, sells or destroys them, as ordered by the court. See §13-3105 for the letter of the law.

Anyone making a lawful arrest may take weapons from the person arrested, and must turn the weapons over to the courts. See §13-3895 for the letter of the law.

Certain weapons are contraband if unregistered and are subject to seizure by the authorities. Included are weapons identified under the National Firearms Act as amended, or identified as prohibited weapons under state law.

Personal property, including firearms and ammunition, may be seized by the Bureau of Alcohol, Tobacco and Firearms when used or intended to be used or involved in violation of any U.S. laws which ATF agents are empowered to enforce. Acquittal or dismissal of charges allows you to regain any confiscated property.

Transport and Shipping

"Guns can be shipped and transported around the country."

You may have a weapon shipped to a licensed dealer, manufacturer or repair shop and back. However, depending upon the reason for the shipment and the shipper being used, the weapon may have to be shipped from and back to someone with a federal firearms license. You should check with the intended recipient and you must inform the shipping agent before shipping firearms.

Any purchased gun which is shipped interstate must go from a licensed dealer to a licensed dealer. Many dealers in the state will act as a "receiving station" for a weapon you purchase elsewhere, sometimes for a fee.

If you buy a gun from a private party out of state, the gun may only be shipped to a licensed dealer within Arizona. If you sell a gun to a private party out of state, the gun must be shipped via a licensed dealer in the purchaser's state.

The only time when you may directly receive an interstate shipment of a gun is the return of a gun which you sent for repairs, modification or replacement to a licensee in another state.

Personal transport of firearms into other states is subject to the laws of each state you are in. Federal law guarantees the right to transport a gun in a private vehicle, if you are entitled to have the gun in your home state and the gun is unloaded and locked in the trunk, or in a locked compartment other than the glove compartment or the console if the vehicle has no trunk.

The authorities have been known to detain or arrest people who are legally travelling with weapons, due to confusion, ignorance and for other reasons. Travelling with personal firearms presents certain risks.

Federal Facilities

Knowingly having a gun or other dangerous weapon (except a pocket knife with a blade under 2½ inches) in a federal facility is punishable by a fine and up to one year imprisonment. Exceptions include authorities performing their duties, possession while hunting, or other lawful purpose. You cannot be convicted unless notice of the law is posted at each public entrance, or if you had actual notice of the law. A federal facility is a building (or part), federally leased or owned, where federal employees regularly work.

A Note About Youngsters

A person under the age of fourteen when an offense occurs cannot be charged criminally for a shooting, unless there is clear proof that the person knew the conduct was wrong when it took place. Also, a person cannot be criminally charged if they suffer from a mental disease or defect which prevents them from either knowing what they are doing, or knowing that what they are doing is wrong.

HUNTING REGULATIONS

Hunting regulations are complex, highly detailed and mandatory requirements issued annually by the Arizona Game and Fish Department (AGFD). The regulations are based on *Arizona Revised Statutes, Title 17.* You *must* get in touch with AGFD before even considering hunting or shooting at any wildlife. *The Arizona Gun Owner's Guide* only covers those parts of hunting rules which apply to firearms use.

The Arizona Game and Fish Department offers a 20-hour course of instruction which teaches safe handling of firearms, ethics and responsibilities, wildlife management and identification, survival, first aid and more. The course includes class and field work, and is open to anyone who is 10 years of age or older.

Land open to hunt is not always open to all shooting. Two small parts of Tonto National Forest, for example, are closed to all shooting *except* licensed hunting. Some land which may be hunted, like the 14-million-plus acres of the Navajo Indian Reservation for example, has a prohibition against firearms altogether.

Here are the key rules about using guns while hunting. Remember that hunting regulations are not limited to guns, and include bow and arrow and other devices.

- The Arizona Game and Fish Department specifies the types of guns and ammunition which are allowed when hunting each different type of game. The specifications are designed to help insure a quick, clean kill. Different types of game may only be hunted in specified areas during specified seasons. It is illegal to otherwise hunt. Main hunting areas are on land regulated by the U.S. Forest Service, the Bureau of Land Management, the State Land Department, Indian Country and private land.

- No one under ten years of age may hunt big game.

- No one between ten and fourteen years of age may hunt big game without having passed the Arizona Hunter Education Course offered by AGFD.

- A person between the ages of ten and fourteen may hunt wildlife other than big game without a license, if accompanied by a properly licensed hunter who is 18 years or older. There is a limit of two children per license holder.

- Anyone over 14 years of age needs a license to hunt wildlife.

- When hunting, you must have in your possession either a Class G General Hunting License, a Class F Combination Hunting and Fishing license, or a Class H Three-Day Hunting License (not valid for big game), plus any required tags, permit tags, or stamps.

- It's illegal to shoot while taking wildlife within a quarter mile of an occupied or possibly occupied farmhouse, cabin, lodge, trailer home or other building, without the permission of the owner or resident.

- It's illegal to shoot from a vehicle while hunting. Special rules apply to hunting waterfowl.

- It's illegal to shoot from, across or into a road or railroad while hunting.

- It's illegal to be intoxicated while hunting.

- It's illegal to handle or fire a gun in a careless or reckless manner while hunting, or with wanton disregard for the safety of human life or property.

- A person involved in a shooting accident while hunting must:
  1 - Render every possible assistance to the injured person;
  2 - Immediately report the accident to and cooperate with the nearest law enforcement officer;
  3 - File a written report of the incident within 10 days to the Arizona Game and Fish Department.

- Poaching (hunting outside of the established regulations) is illegal and strongly discouraged. To anonymously report a suspected violation, call Operation Game Thief, 1-800-352-0700, 24 hours a day.

  Rewards are anonymously paid for tips leading to arrests through the Operation Game Thief program, by AGFD and these organizations: Arizona Bowhunters Association, Tucson Rod and Gun Club, Arizona Desert Bighorn Sheep Society, Arizona Bowhunters and Field Archers Association, *Western Bowhunter* Magazine, Arizona Muzzleloading Association, Western Bowhunters Association, Central Arizona Bowhunters, Sportsman's Voice, Phoenix Varmint Callers and the Arizona Trapper's Association. Rewards can be as high as $1,000.

- It's illegal to have a gun for taking game within a game refuge, without special written consent of the Arizona Game and Fish Commission.

- Legal shooting time while hunting is during daylight hours. Weather conditions can alter actual times - you must be able to see well enough to shoot safely, to be legal. A few special exceptions apply.

- It's illegal to destroy, injure or molest livestock, growing crops, personal property, notices or signboards, or other improvements while hunting.

- It's illegal to shoot an animal and let any edible meat go to waste. Abandoning a carcass is illegal.

- Tracer ammunition, armor-piercing or full-jacketed bullets designed for military use are not allowed.

- Machine guns and silencers are not allowed.

- Semi-automatic centerfire rifles with a magazine capacity of more than five rounds are not allowed.

- Poisoned or explosive projectiles are not allowed.

- Shotguns larger than 10-gauge, or shotguns capable of holding more than two shells in the magazine are not allowed. Larger capacity shotguns must be plugged to limit the magazine to 2 shells.

- The use or possession of lead shot is prohibited in areas designated as nontoxic shot zones.

- Hunting with rifled firearms is prohibited within the Maricopa County Parks System. Limited deer hunting with rifled firearms, by special permit, may be allowed for a limited time by the Maricopa County Park Commission in cooperation with the Arizona Game and Fish Commission.

- Rifled firearms are prohibited in the Base and Meridian Wildlife Areas, and centerfire rifled firearms are prohibited in the Robbins Butte Wildlife Area. Many other Wildlife Area restrictions apply.

- A person participating in "archery-only" season may not use or possess a firearm.

- A person participating in "handguns, archery, and muzzle-loader (HAM)" season may not use or possess a long gun except a muzzle-loader.

- A special permit is available from the Phoenix office of AGFD which allows a physically disabled person to shoot from a motor vehicle, if a) the vehicle has a current handicapped license plate or disabled shooter's permit, b) is standing still, c) is not on a maintained public roadway, d) has its engine off, and e) is not used at any time to hunt or pursue wildlife.

Hunting Penalties

- Hunting license privileges may be revoked for up to five years for careless use of firearms resulting in human injury or death, destroying or injuring livestock, unlawful taking or possession of wildlife, or acts of vandalism.

- Unless a penalty is otherwise specifically described by law, violation of hunting regulations is a class 2 misdemeanor.

- Knowingly taking, having or transporting big game unlawfully is a class 1 misdemeanor.

- Knowingly selling, bartering or offering for sale any big game which was taken unlawfully is a class 6 felony.

- Any peace officer who knowingly fails to enforce a hunting regulation is guilty of a class 2 misdemeanor.

- Anyone who unlawfully wounds, kills or has possession of certain wildlife is subject to civil suit by the Arizona Game and Fish Department in addition to other penalties. The list includes any endangered species, elk, bighorn sheep, buffalo, all eagles, deer, antelope, mountain lion, bear, turkey, javelina, beaver, goose, raptors, duck, small game animals, small game birds, game fish and non-game birds.

NOTES ON FEDERAL LAW

Dealers of firearms must be licensed by the Bureau of Alcohol, Tobacco and Firearms. Federal law requires that licensed dealers of firearms must keep records of each sale. This information is permanently saved by the dealer, but is otherwise unreported.

"Unreported" means there's no central place for anyone to check and see if a given individual owns a firearm. The only person who knows is the person who sells you a firearm. For someone else to find out if you have a gun, they would have to check all the records of all the dealers in the country, a daunting task. Only the Bureau of Alcohol, Tobacco and Firearms (ATF) is authorized to check the records of manufacture, importation and sale of firearms.

The dealer's records allow guns to be *traced*, a very different and important matter. When a gun is involved in a crime, ATF can find out, from the manufacturer's serial number, which licensed dealer originally received the gun. The dealer can then look through the records and see who purchased the weapon. It's a one-way street - a gun can be linked to a purchaser but owners can't be traced to their guns. One study of successful traces showed that 4 out of 5 were of some value to law enforcement authorities.

When President Reagan was shot by John Hinckley Jr., the weapon was traced and in fourteen minutes time, a retail sale to Hinckley was confirmed.

Buying, selling, having, making, transferring and transporting guns are in many cases regulated by federal laws. These regulations are covered in *The Arizona Gun Owner's Guide*, but for the most part, only state penalties are noted. There may be federal penalties as well.

Under the Assimilative Crimes Act, state law controls if there is no federal law covering a situation. Murder is a typical example of this. It is important to recognize that there can be a question of jurisdiction in some cases.

A long history of federal regulation exists with regard to firearms and other weapons. The main laws include:

- Second Amendment to the Constitution (1789)
- National Firearms Act (1934)
- Federal Firearms Act (1938)
- Omnibus Crime Control and Safe Streets Act (1968)
- Gun Control Act (1968)
- Organized Crime Control Act (1970)
- Omnibus Crime Control Act (1986)
- Firearm Owner's Protection Act (1986)

Additional federal requirements may be found in the Code of Federal Regulations and the United States Code.

WHAT'S WRONG WITH THIS PICTURE?

These weapons and destructive devices are illegal unless they are pre-registered with the Bureau of Alcohol, Tobacco and Firearms.

- A rifle with a barrel less than 16 inches long
- A shotgun with a barrel less than 18 inches long
- A modified rifle or shotgun less than 26 inches overall
- Machine guns or machine pistols
- Silencers of any kind
- Firearms using fixed ammunition over .50 caliber
- Armor-piercing ammunition
- Explosive, incendiary or poison gas bombs
- Explosive, incendiary or poison gas grenades
- Explosive, incendiary or poison gas mines
- Explosive, incendiary or poison gas rockets with more than 4 ounces of propellant (includes bazooka)
- Missiles with an explosive or incendiary charge greater than 1/4 ounce
- Mortars

GUN SAFETY AND USE 5

Many fine books and classes exist which teach the current wisdom on gun safety and use. In Arizona, some of the best public classes are given by the Arizona Game and Fish Department and the Arizona State Rifle and Pistol Association.

When studying firearm safety (and every gun owner should), you will no doubt come across the Ten Commandments of Gun Safety. These well-intentioned lists have serious drawbacks - no two lists are ever the same and there are many more than ten rules to follow for safe gun use. In addition, hunters must learn many rules which don't apply to other shooters. For instance, a hunter should never openly carry game - it makes you an unwitting target of other hunters.

The Commandments of Safety are actually a way of saying, "Here's how people have accidents with guns." Each rule implies a kind of mishap. It's good exercise to look at each rule and read between the lines to find its counterpart - the potential disaster the rule will help you avoid. For example, rule number 1 translates into, "People have accidents with guns which they think are empty." Always keep in mind the prime directive: Take time to be safe instead of forever being sorry.

THE GUN OWNER'S COMMANDMENTS OF SAFETY

1 - Treat every gun as if it is loaded until you have personally proven otherwise.

2 - Always keep a gun pointed in a safe direction.

3 - Never point a gun at anything you do not intend to shoot.

4 - Don't touch the trigger until you're ready to fire.

5 - Be certain of your target and what is beyond it before pulling the trigger.

6 - Use but never rely on the safety.

7 - Never load a gun until ready to use. Unload a gun immediately after use.

8 - Only use ammunition which exactly matches the markings on your gun.

9 - Always read and follow manufacturers' instructions carefully.

10 - Always wear adequate eye and ear protection when shooting.

11 - If a gun fails to fire:
  a) keep it pointed in a safe direction
  b) wait thirty seconds in case of a delayed firing
  c) unload the gun carefully, avoiding exposure to the breech.

12 - Don't climb fences or trees, or jump logs or ditches with a chambered round.

13 - Be able to control the direction of the muzzle even if you stumble.

14 - Keep the barrel and action clear of obstructions.

15 - Avoid carrying ammunition which doesn't match the gun you are carrying.

16 - Be aware that customized guns may require ammunition which doesn't match the gun's original markings.

17 - Store guns with the action open.

18 - Store ammunition and guns separately, and out of reach of children and careless adults.

19 - Never pull a gun toward you by the muzzle.

20 - Never horseplay with a firearm.

21 - Never shoot at a hard flat surface, or at water, to prevent ricochets.

22 - Be sure you have an adequate backstop for target shooting.

23 - At a shooting range, always keep a gun pointed downrange.

24 - Always obey a range officer's commands immediately.

25 - On open terrain with other people present, keep guns pointed upwards, or downwards and away from the people.

26 - Never handle a gun you are not familiar with.

27 - Learn to operate a gun empty before attempting to load and shoot it.

28 - Never transport a loaded firearm in a vehicle.

29 - Never lean a firearm where it may slip and fall.

30 - Do not use alcohol or mood-altering drugs when you are handling firearms.

31 - When loading or unloading a firearm, always keep the muzzle pointed in a safe direction.

THERE'S NOTHING WRONG WITH THIS PICTURE!

THERE'S NOTHING WRONG
WITH THIS PICTURE!

Practicing the shooting sports outdoors is all right as long as you comply with the laws.

- The shooters are at a remote location, on land which isn't restricted.
- The target leaves no debris.
- The target has a backstop which prevents bullets from causing a potential hazard.
- No wildlife or protected plants are in the line of fire.
- The shooters are using eye and ear protection.

32 - Never use a rifle scope instead of a pair of binoculars.

33 - Always remember that removing the clip from semi-automatic and automatic weapons may still leave a live round, ready to fire, in the chamber.

34 - Never rely on one empty cylinder next to the barrel of a revolver as a guarantee of safety, since different revolvers rotate in opposite directions.

35 - Never step into a boat holding a loaded firearm.

36 - It's difficult to use a gun safely until you become a marksman.

37 - It's difficult to handle a gun safely if you need corrective lenses and are not wearing them.

38 - Know the effective range and the maximum range of a firearm and the ammunition you are using.

39 - Be sure that anyone with access to a firearm kept in a home understands its safe use.

40 - Don't fire a large caliber weapon if you cannot control the recoil.

41 - Never put your finger in the trigger guard when drawing a gun from a holster.

42 - Never put your hand in front of the cylinder of a revolver when firing.

43 - Always leave the hammer of a revolver resting over an empty chamber.

44 - Never put your hand in back of the slide of a semi-automatic pistol when firing.

45 - Never leave ammunition around when cleaning a gun.

46 - Clean firearms after they have been used. A dirty gun is not as safe as a clean one.

47 - Never fire a blank round directly at a person. Blanks can blind, maim, and at close range, they can kill.

48 - Only use modern firearms in good working condition, and ammunition which is fresh.

49 - Accidents don't happen, they are caused, and it's up to you and you alone to prevent them in all cases. Every "accident" which ever happened could have been avoided. Where there are firearms there is a need for caution.

50 - Always think first and shoot second.

HOW WELL DO YOU KNOW YOUR GUN?

Safe and effective use of firearms demands that you understand your weapon thoroughly. This knowledge is best gained through a combination of reading, classes and practice with a qualified instructor. The simple test below will help tell you if you are properly trained in the use of firearms. If you're not sure what all the terms mean, can you be absolutely sure that you're qualified to handle firearms safely?

☐ Action	☐ Firing Pin	☐ Primer
☐ Ammunition	☐ Firing Line	☐ Projectile
☐ Automatic	☐ Forearm	☐ Prone
☐ Ballistics	☐ Fouling	☐ Pump Action
☐ Barrel	☐ Frame	☐ Pyrodex
☐ Black Powder	☐ Gauge	☐ Receiver
☐ Bolt	☐ Grip	☐ Repeater
☐ Bore	☐ Grip Panels	☐ Revolver
☐ Break Action	☐ Grooves	☐ Rifle
☐ Breech	☐ Gunpowder	☐ Rifling
☐ Buckshot	☐ Half Cock	☐ Rimfire
☐ Bullet	☐ Hammer	☐ Safety
☐ Butt	☐ Handgun	☐ Sear
☐ Caliber	☐ Hangfire	☐ Semi-Automatic
☐ Cartridge	☐ Hunter Orange	☐ Shell
☐ Case	☐ Ignition	☐ Shooting Positions
☐ Casing	☐ Kneeling	☐ Shot
☐ Centerfire	☐ Lands	☐ Shotgun
☐ Chamber	☐ Lever Action	☐ Sights
☐ Checkering	☐ Magazine	☐ Sighting-In
☐ Choke	☐ Mainspring	☐ Sitting
☐ Clip	☐ Maximum Range	☐ Smokeless Powder
☐ Cock	☐ Misfire	☐ Smoothbore
☐ Comb	☐ Muzzle	☐ Standing
☐ Cylinder	☐ Muzzleloader	☐ Stock
☐ Discharge	☐ Pattern	☐ Trigger
☐ Dominant Eye	☐ Pistol	☐ Trigger Guard
☐ Effective Range	☐ Powder	☐ Unplugged Shotgun
☐ Firearm		

**It is the responsibility
of every American
to prevent firearms from being
instruments of tragedy.**

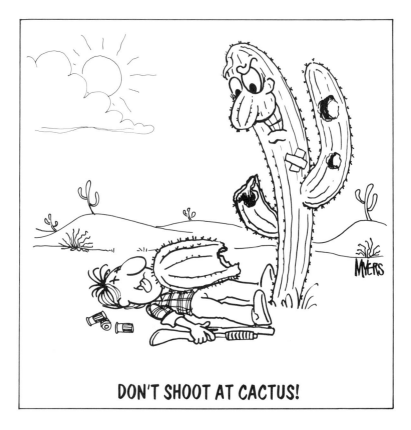

DON'T SHOOT AT CACTUS!

DON'T SHOOT AT CACTUS!

Cactus is a treasure which the state of Arizona is lucky to have. They are legally protected plants - it's a crime to shoot at them or harm them in any way. Removing any cactus from the desert without special authorization is against the law. Only the lowest and sleaziest dregs of society would even think of shooting at these harmless and majestic natives of the state.

Cactus can't shoot back, but there's at least one case on record of a cactus that got even!

THE APPENDIX

APPENDIX A
GLOSSARY OF TERMS

ACT = A bodily movement.

ADEQUATE PROVOCATION = Conduct or circumstances sufficient to make a reasonable person lose self-control.

ARREST = To deprive a person of liberty by legal authority.

B•B GUN = A gun designed to forcibly propel a ball, pellet, dart or other projectile using compressed gas or a spring mechanism.

BENEFIT = Anything of value or advantage, now or in the future.

BIG GAME = Antelope, bear, bison (buffalo), deer, elk, mountain lion, peccary (javelina), bighorn sheep and wild turkey.

CONDUCT = The actions you take or refrain from, and your thoughts about them.

CRIME = A felony, misdemeanor or petty offense.

CRIMINAL NEGLIGENCE = Failure to recognize a risk so dangerous that a reasonable person would be expected to recognize it.

CULPABLE MENTAL STATE = An accountable state of mind. Specifically: intentionally, knowingly, recklessly or with criminal negligence, in the senses described by law.

DANGEROUS DRUG = For a detailed description, see Arizona Revised Statutes, §13-3401.

DANGEROUS INSTRUMENT = Anything which can readily be used to cause death or serious physical injury.

DEADLY PHYSICAL FORCE = Force which can cause death or serious physical injury.

DEADLY WEAPON = Anything designed for lethal use. The term includes a firearm.

DEAL = To engage in the business of selling firearms at wholesale or to repair or modify firearms, with the principal objective of making a livelihood or profit.

DEFACE = To remove, alter or destroy the manufacturer's serial number.

ENTERPRISE = A corporation, association, labor union or other legal entity.

EXPLOSIVE = Dynamite, nitroglycerine, black powder, plastic explosive or other similar materials. Ammunition and hand-loading ammunition supplies are excluded.

FELONY = A serious crime. An offense against the law which carries a sentence of imprisonment under the custody of the state Department of Corrections. Felony prison sentences run from 1½ years to life imprisonment with no chance of parole until 25 years have been served. A class 1 felony (1st degree murder) carries a possible sentence of death. Arizona uses the gas chamber to inflict the penalty of death. Felony fines may be up to $150,000 for an individual, and up to $1,000,000 for an enterprise.

FIREARM = Any loaded or unloaded pistol, revolver, rifle, shotgun or other weapon which can fire a projectile by using an explosive. A permanently inoperable firearm is excluded.

GOVERNMENT = The recognized political structure.

GOVERNMENT FUNCTION = Any activity which a public servant is authorized to do for the government.

GUN = A firearm.

HOMICIDE = First or second degree murder, manslaughter or negligent homicide.

ILLEGAL = Unlawful. An offense. A crime.

INTENTIONALLY or WITH THE INTENT TO = With the objective of causing a specific result.

INTOXICATION = Mental or physical incapacity caused by drugs, toxic vapors or alcohol.

JUSTIFICATION = Legal right to shoot a person.

KNOWINGLY = With awareness of your conduct and situation.

LAW = Formal rules by which society controls itself. In Arizona, the law means the Arizona Revised Statutes. Cities and other governments within the state may not enact a law which contradicts state law.

LESSEE = A person who leases something from another person.

MACHINE GUN = A firearm capable of shooting more than one shot automatically, by a single pull of the trigger.

MISDEMEANOR = A crime less serious than a felony. An offense against the law which carries a sentence of imprisonment in a local facility, not to the state Department of Corrections. Misdemeanor jail sentences run up to six months. Misdemeanor fines can run up to $1,000 for an individual, and up to $20,000 for an enterprise.

NARCOTIC DRUG = For a detailed description, see Arizona Revised Statutes, §13-3401.

OFFENSE = Any conduct described in the law which carries a jail sentence or fine. A crime.

OMISSION = Failure to do something required by law.

PEACE OFFICER = Anyone with legal authority to maintain public order and make arrests.

PERSON = A human being, or, as applicable, an enterprise or government.

PETTY OFFENSE = A minor criminal violation. An offense against the law which carries only a fine as a penalty. Petty offenses run up to $300 for an individual, and up to $1000 for an enterprise.

PHYSICAL FORCE = Force used on another person. Confining another person is considered physical force.

PHYSICAL INJURY = Harm to the physical condition of a person or property.

POACHING = Hunting illegally, by either hunting without a valid license, outside of regulations, taking wildlife during closed season or possessing unlawfully taken wildlife.

POSSESS = To knowingly have or exercise control over property.

POSSESSION = The voluntary act of exercising control over property.

PREMEDITATION = Acting with the intention or knowledge that you will kill another human being. The intention or knowledge must preceed the killing by a length of time sufficient to permit reflection. Killing in the instant effect of a sudden quarrel or heat of passion is not premeditation.

PROHIBITED POSSESSOR = A person who is not allowed to have a gun. See Chapter 1 for a detailed description.

PROHIBITED WEAPON = Guns and other weapons which are a crime to have, make, sell, transport or transfer without federal registration. A National Firearms Act (NFA) weapon. See Chapter 2 for a detailed description.

PROPERTY = Anything of tangible or intangible value.

PUBLIC SERVANT = Any officer or employee of any branch of government. Public servants may be elected, appointed, or hired. Consultants working for government and peace officers are included. Jurors and witnesses are excluded. You become a public servant at the time you are selected, which may be before you actually occupy the specific government position.

REASONABLE = This term is used to describe behavior and circumstances which fit into a generally recognized and accepted norm. It is frequently possible to argue about the precise meaning of the word, depending on the situation.

REASONABLE PERSON = An imaginary person who conforms to generally recognized and accepted norms.

RECKLESSLY = With awareness of and disregard for a risk so dangerous that a reasonable person would not ignore it.

RIFLED BARREL = A gun barrel with internal grooves for giving the bullet a spin which helps stabilize it in flight. Rifled weapons are restricted in limited areas, notably the Maricopa County Parks. Most handguns are rifled.

SERIOUS PHYSICAL INJURY = Injury which creates a reasonable risk of death. Also, injury which causes serious and permanent disfigurement, loss of any organ or limb, or serious long-term harm to health, an organ or a limb.

TAKING = Pursuing, shooting, hunting, fishing, trapping, killing, capturing, snaring or netting wildlife, or placing any device to capture or kill wildlife.

TRANSFER = Sell, assign, pledge, lease, loan, give away or otherwise dispose of.

UNLAWFUL = Against the law. Illegal. A crime.

VEHICLE = Any device used for transportation of people or property, on a road, waterway, airway or off-road. Devices using solely human power, and devices which travel on tracks or rails are excluded.

VOLUNTARY ACT = A deliberate bodily movement.

VOLUNTARY INTOXICATION = Getting drunk or high on alcohol, drugs or toxic vapors which you know, or should know, will cause the effect. Taking alcohol, drugs or toxic vapors under medical advice is excluded. Taking such substances under duress may afford a defense.

APPENDIX B

CRIME AND PUNISHMENT CHART

Explanations

TYPE OF CRIME: Illegal activities are divided into these ten categories, to match the punishment to the crime.

JAIL: These are the sentences for a first offense. A class 1 felony, in addition to life imprisonment with no chance of parole for at least 25 years, carries a possible death penalty. For class 4, 5 or 6 felonies, sentences may be raised by up to 25% or reduced by up to 50%, depending on circumstances. For class 2 and 3 felonies, sentences may be raised by up to 100% or decreased by up to 25%, depending on circumstances. Misdemeanor jail terms may range from zero to the maximum, determined by the court.

FINE: These are the maximums, listed for individuals/ enterprises. Fines are payable immediately, but a court may grant permission to pay by a certain date, or in installments. The letter "M" in this column indicates "thousand," and the letters "MM" indicate "million."

TIME LIMIT: Frequently called "the statute of limitations." The period of time, from the discovery of an offense (or from the time when an offense should have been discovered with the exercise of reasonable diligence), within which a prosecution may begin. When a class 2, 3 or 4 felony involves homicide there is no time limit. The period of limitation is put on hold if you are out of state, or if you have no known abode within the state. Bargaining a class 6 felony to a misdemeanor does not change the time limit.

TYPICAL OFFENSE: This is only a partial list of offenses.

CRIME AND PUNISHMENT

These are the maximum penalties for a first offense. Included are some typical crimes within each category. See the accompanying notes on the facing page.

TYPE OF CRIME	JAIL	FINE	TIME LIMIT
Class 1 Felony	For Life	$150M/$1MM	None
First degree murder.			
Class 2 Felony	7 years	$150M/$1MM	7 years
Second degree murder, bringing a gun into a prison.			
Class 3 Felony	5 years	$150M/$1MM	7 years
Manslaughter, assisting a suicide, aggravated assault.			
Class 4 Felony	4 years	$150M/$1MM	7 years
Negligent homicide, possession or sale of a prohibited weapon.			
Class 5 Felony	2 years	$150M/$1MM	7 years
Bringing a gun into or around a juvenile correctional facility, any unclassified felony in state law.			
Class 6 Felony	1½ years	$150M/$1MM	7 years
Endangerment with a risk of death, defacing a gun, possessing a defaced gun, providing a gun to a prohibited possessor, possession of a gun by a prohibited possessor, unlawful sale of big game.			
Class 1 Misdemeanor	6 months	$1M/$20M	1 year
Concealing a weapon on yourself or in a car, refusing to leave or check deadly weapons at a public place or event when asked, entering a polling place armed, endangerment without a risk of death, threatening or intimidating, disorderly conduct, poaching big game.			
Class 2 Misdemeanor	4 months	$750/$10M	1 year
Transferring firearms to a minor without written consent from parent or guardian, shooting within city limits, bringing a gun into a bar, threatened assault, most hunting violations, any unclassified misdemeanor in state law.			
Class 3 Misdemeanor	30 days	$500/$2M	1 year
Failure to report gunshot wound, physically provoking someone.			
Petty Offense	None	$300/$1M	6 months
Any offense not classified as a felony or misdemeanor.			

APPENDIX C

THE PROPER AUTHORITIES

Regulations on guns and their use come from a lot of places. Listed with each authority are the addresses and phones of the nearest offices. All phone numbers are in area code (602) and all cities are in Arizona (AZ) unless indicated.

Arizona Commission on Indian Affairs 542-3123
1645 W. Jefferson; Phoenix 85007

> **Ak-Chin Reservation -**
> **Ak-Chin Indian Community 568-2221**
> Route 2, Box 27; Maricopa 85239

> **Camp Verde Reservation -**
> **Yavapai-Apache Indian Community 567-3649**
> P.O. Box 1188, Camp Verde 86322

> **Cocopah Reservation -**
> **Cocopah Tribe 627-2102**
> Bin G, Somerton 85350

> **Colorado River Reservation -**
> **Colorado River Indian Tribes 669-9211**
> Route 1, Box 23-B, Parker 85344

> **Fort Apache Reservation -**
> **White Mountain Apache Tribe 338-4346**
> P.O. Box 1150, Whiteriver 85941

> **Fort McDowell Reservation -**
> **Mohave-Apache Tribe 990-0995**
> P.O. Box 17779, Fountain Hills 85268

> **Fort Mojave Reservation -**
> **Fort Mojave Tribe (619) 326-4591**
> 500 Merriman Avenue, Needles, CA 92363

Fort Yuma Reservation -
Quechan Tribe (619) 572-0213
P.O. Box 11352, Yuma 85366

Gila River Reservation -
Gila River Indian Community 562-3311
P.O. Box 97, Sacaton 85247

Havasupai Reservation -
Havasupai Tribe 448-2731
P.O. Box 10, Supai 86435

Hopi Reservation -
Hopi Tribe 734-2441
P.O. Box 123, Kyakotsmovi 86039

Hualapai Reservation -
Hualapai Tribe 769-2216
P.O. Box 168, Peach Springs 86434

Kaibab-Paiute Reservation -
Kaibab-Paiute Tribe 643-7245
Tribal Affairs Building, Fredonia 86022

Navajo Reservation -
The Navajo Tribe 871-4941
P.O. Box 308, Window Rock 86515

Pascua Yaqui Reservation -
Pascua Yaqui Tribe 883-2838
7474 S. Camino de Oeste, Tucson 85746

Salt River Reservation -
Salt River Pima-Maricopa Indian Community
941-7277 Route 1, Box 216, Scottsdale 85256

San Carlos Reservation -
San Carlos Apache Tribe 475-2361
P.O. Box "O", San Carlos 85550

Tohono O'Odham Reservation -
Tohono O'Odham Tribe 383-2221
P.O. Box 837, Sells 85634

Tonto Apache Reservation -
Tonto Apache Tribe 474-5000
#30 Tonto Apache Reservation, Payson 85547

**Yavapai-Prescott Reservation -
Yavapai-Prescott Tribe 445-8790**
530 E. Merritt Street, Prescott 86301

Arizona Game and Fish Department (AGFD) 942-3000
2222   West Greenway Road; Phoenix 85034

> **AGFD Region I 367-4342**
> HC 62, Box 57201; Pinetop 89535
>
> **AGFD Region II 774-5045**
> 3500 Lake Mary Road; Flagstaff 86001
>
> **AGFD Region III 692-7700**
> 5325 Stockton Hill Road; Kingman 86401
>
> **AGFD Region IV 342-0091**
> 3005 Pacific Avenue; Yuma 85365
>
> **AGFD Region V 628-5376**
> 555 North Greasewood; Tucson 85745
>
> **AGFD Region VI 981-9400**
> 7200 E. University; Mesa 85207

Arizona State Land Department 542-4621
1616 W. Adams; Phoenix 85007

Arizona State Parks 542-4174
800 W. Washington #415, Phoenix 85007

> **Alamo Lake State Park 669-2088**
> 38 mi. north of Wenden and US 60
>
> **Boyce Thompson Southwestern
> Arboretum 689-2811**
> 3 mi. west of Superior on US 60
>
> **Buckskin Mountain State Park 667-3231**
> 11 mi. north of Parker on AZ 95
>
> **Catalina State Park 628-5798**
> 9 mi. north of Tucson on US 89
>
> **Dead Horse Ranch State Park 634-5283**
> Across river from Cottonwood, enter on north
> 5th Street

Fort Verde State Historic Park 567-3275
In Camp Verde, 3 mi. east of I-17

Homolovi Ruins State Park 289-4106
5 mi. east of Winslow off Highway 87

Jerome State Historic Park 634-5381
In Jerome, off US 89A

Kartchner Caverns State Park
P.O. Box 1849, Benson

Lake Havasu State Park Windsor Beach 855-7851
Off AZ 95, in Lake Havasu City

Cattail Cove 855-1223
15 mi. south of Lake Havasu City

Lost Dutchman State Park 982-4485
5 mi. northeast of Apache Junction on AZ 88

Lyman Lake State Park 337-4441
11 mi. south of St. Johns; 1 mi. east of US 666

McFarland Historical State Park 868-5216
In Florence, off US 89 and AZ 287

Oracle State Park 896-2425
1 mi. east of Oracle off the old Mt. Lemmon Rd.

Painted Rocks State Park 683-2151
15 mi. west and 12 mi. north of Gila Bend

Patagonia Lake State Park 287-6965
12 mi. northeast of Nogales on AZ 82

Picacho Peak State Park 466-3183
40 mi. north of Tucson on I-10

Red Rock State Park 282-6907
South of Sedona, off Red Rock Loop Rd.

Riordan State Historic Park 779-4395
In Flagstaff, off Riordan Ranch St.

Roper Lake State Park 428-6760
6 mi. south of Safford; ½ mi. east of US 666

Slide Rock State Park 282-3034
7 mi. north of Sedona on 89A

**Tombstone Courthouse State
Historic Park 457-3311**
In Tombstone, off US 80

Tubac Presidio State Historic Park 398-2252
In Tubac, off I-19

**Yuma Territorial Prison State
Historic Park 783-4771, 343-2500**
In Yuma, off I-8

Arizona State Rifle and Pistol Association 838-6064
1727 E. Alameda, Tempe 85282

**Bureau of Alcohol, Tobacco and
Firearms (202) 927-8410**
650 Massachusetts Avenue, NW; Washington, DC 20226

**Bureau of Alcohol, Tobacco and Firearms
Arizona Office 640-2025, 2938**
201 E. Indianola; Phoenix 85012

Bureau of Indian Affairs (202) 208-7163
1849 C. Street, NW; Washington, DC 20240

Bureau of Indian Affairs Arizona Office 379-6600
1 N. 1st St.; P.O. Box 10; Phoenix 85001

Bureau of Land Management (BLM) (202) 343-5717
U.S. Dept. of Interior; 18th & C St. NW; Wash., DC 20240

BLM Arizona State Office 640-5504
3707 N. 7th Street; Phoenix 85014

BLM Arizona Strip District Office (801) 673-3545
390 N. 3050 E.; St. George, UT 84770

BLM Havasu Resource Area Office 855-8017
3189 Sweetwater Avenue; Lake Havasu City 86403

BLM Kingman Resource Area Office 757-3161
2475 Beverly Avenue; Kingman 86401

BLM Phoenix District Office 863-4464
2015 W. Deer Valley Rd.; Phoenix 85027

BLM Safford District Office 428-4040
425 E. 4th Street; Safford 85546

BLM Yuma District Office 762-6300
3150 Winsor Avenue; Yuma 85365

County Parks and Recreation Departments (P&RD)

Coconino County P&RD 779-5130
100 E. Birch, Flagstaff 86001

Maricopa County P&RD 506-2930
3475 W. Durango, Phoenix 85009

Mohave County P&RD 753-0739
P.O. Box 7000, Kingman 86401

Navajo County P&RD 524-3094
P.O. Box 668, Holbrook 86025

Pima County P&RD 740-2680
1204 W. Silver Lake Road, Tucson 85713

Yavapai County P&RD 771-3321
County Courthouse, Room 107, Prescott 86301

Lawyer Referral 257-4434
333 W. Roosevelt, Phoenix 85003

National Park Service 640-5250
202 E. Earll #115, Phoenix 85012

Canyon de Chelly National Monument 674-5436
Box 588, Chinle 86503

Casa Grande Ruins National Monument 723-3172
1100 Ruins Drive, Coolidge 85228

**Chiracahua National Monument
824-3560 or 824-3460**
Wilcox 85643

Glen Canyon National Recreation Area 645-2471
Box 1507, Page 86040

Grand Canyon National Park 638-7888
Box 129, Grand Canyon 86023

**Lake Mead National
Recreation Area (702) 293-8920**
601 Nevada Highway, Boulder City, NV 89005

Montezuma Castle National Monument 567-3322
P.O. Box 219, Campe Verde 86322

Navajo National Monument 672-2366
Tonalea 86044

Organ Pipe Cactus National Monument 387-6849
Route 1, Box 100, Ajo 85321

Petrified Forest National Park 524-6228
Petrified Forest National Park 86028

Pipe Springs National Monument (801) 643-5505
c/o Zion National Park, Springdale, UT 84767

Saguaro National Monument 670-6680
Old Spanish Trail, Rt. 8, Box 695, Tucson 85730

Sunset Crater National Monument 527-7042
Route 3, Box 149, Flagstaff 86004

Tonto National Monument 467-2241
Box 707, Roosevelt 85545

Tumacacori National Monument 398-2341
Box 67, Tumacacori 85640

Tuzigoot National Monument 634-5564
Box 219, Camp Verde 86322

Walnut Canyon National Monument 526-3367
Walnut Canyon Road, Flagstaff 86004

Wupatki National Monument 527-7040
HC 33, Box 444A, Flagstaff 86004

National Rifle Association (800) 336-7402
1600 Rhode Island Avenue NW, Washington, DC 20036

Secretary of State (Arizona) 542-4285
Capitol West Wing, Phoenix 85007

U.S. Forest Service Offices

Forest Service, U.S. Dept. of Agriculture, (202) 655-4000
P.O. Box 96090, Washington, D.C. 20090

Regional Forester (505) 842-3292
Federal Bldg., 517 Gold Avenue,
Albuquerque, NM 87102

Apache National Forest 333-4301, 4372
S. Mountain Avenue, Hwy. 180, P.O. Box 640,
Springerville 85935

Coconino National Forest 556-7400
2323 E. Greenlaw Lane, Flagstaff 86001

Coronado National Forest 670-6483
Federal Bldg., 300 W. Congress, Tucson 85701

Kaibab National Forest 635-2681
800 S. 6th St., Williams 86046

Prescott National Forest 445-1762
344 S. Cortez St., Prescott 86301

Sitgreaves National Forest
Now consolidated with Apache National Forest

Tonto National Forest 225-5200
2324 E. McDowell, Phoenix 85010

APPENDIX D

THE ARIZONA GUN LAWS

On the following pages are excerpts from the *Arizona Revised Statutes, Title 13, The Criminal Code*, reproduced directly from the printed edition issued by the Secretary of State, dated December 1988. This has been updated through January 1, 1992. Title 13 covers all criminal conduct, not just the gun laws. Only the gun laws are included in this appendix. A complete copy of the Criminal Code is available from the Secretary of State.

How State Law Is Arranged

Arizona's laws are covered under 46 separate "titles." Within each title, each piece of law is numbered, starting at 101, and going as high as necessary. Each numbered part is called a "Section," represented by a "§" sign.

This makes it easy to refer to any particular law - just call it by its title and section numbers. For instance, §13-3102 is the part about misconduct with weapons. You say it like this, "title thirteen, section thirty one oh two," or simply, "thirteen thirty one oh two."

Excerpt from the Constitution of the State of Arizona

Section 26. Bearing Arms. The right of the individual citizen to bear arms in defense of himself or the state shall not be impaired, but nothing in this section shall be construed as authorizing individuals or corporations to organize, maintain, or employ an armed body of men.

EXCERPTS FROM THE
ARIZONA REVISED STATUTES
TITLE 13 • CRIMINAL CODE

CHAPTER 1

GENERAL PROVISIONS

13-101. Purposes

It is declared that the public policy of this state and the general purposes of the provisions of this title are:

1. To proscribe conduct that unjustifiably and inexcusably causes or threatens substantial harm to individual or public interests;

2. To give fair warning of the nature of the conduct proscribed and of the sentences authorized upon conviction;

3. To define the act or omission and the accompanying mental state which constitute each offense and limit the condemnation of conduct as criminal when it does not fall within the purposes set forth;

4. To differentiate on reasonable grounds between serious and minor offenses and to prescribe proportionate penalties for each;

5. To insure the public safety by preventing the commission of offenses through the deterrent influence of the sentences authorized; and

6. To impose just and deserved punishment on those whose conduct threatens the public peace.

13-107. Time limitations

A. A prosecution for any homicide, misuse of public monies or a felony involving falsification of public records may be commenced at any time.

B. Except as otherwise provided in this section, prosecutions for other offenses must be commenced within the following periods after actual discovery by the state or the political subdivision having jurisdiction of the offense or discovery by the state or such political subdivision which should have occurred with the exercise of reasonable diligence, whichever first occurs:

1. For a class 2 through a class 6 felony, seven years.

2. For a misdemeanor, one year.

3. For a petty offense, six months.

C. For the purposes of subsection B, a prosecution is commenced when an indictment, information or complaint is filed.

D. The period of limitation does not run during any time when the accused is absent from the state or has no reasonably ascertainable place of abode within the state.

E. The time limitation within which a prosecution of a class 6 felony shall commence shall be determined pursuant to subsection B, paragraph 1, irrespective of whether a court enters a judgment of conviction for or a prosecuting attorney designates such offense as a misdemeanor.

F. If a complaint, indictment or information filed before the period of limitation has expired is dismissed for any reason, a new prosecution may be commenced within six months after the dismissal becomes final even if the period of limitation has expired at the time of the dismissal or will expire within six months of such dismissal.

CHAPTER 4

JUSTIFICATION

13-401. Unavailability of justification defense; justification
         as defense
A. Even though a person is justified under this chapter in
threatening or using physical force or deadly physical force against
another, if in doing so such person recklessly injures or kills an
innocent third person, the justification afforded by this chapter is
unavailable in a prosecution for the reckless injury or killing of the
innocent third person.
B. Except as provided in subsection A, justification, as defined
in this chapter, is a defense in any prosecution for an offense pursuant
to this title.

13-402. Justification; execution of public duty
A. Unless inconsistent with the other sections of this chapter
defining justifiable use of physical force or deadly physical force or
with some other superseding provision of law, conduct which would
otherwise constitute an offense is justifiable when it is required or
authorized by law.
B. The justification afforded by subsection A also applies if:
1. A reasonable person would believe such conduct is required or
authorized by the judgment or direction of a competent court or tribunal
or in the lawful execution of legal process, notwithstanding lack of
jurisdiction of the court or defect in the legal process; or
2. A reasonable person would believe such conduct is required or
authorized to assist a peace officer in the performance of such officer's
duties, notwithstanding that the officer exceeded the officer's legal
authority.

13-403. Justification; use of physical force
The use of physical force upon another person which would
otherwise constitute an offense is justifiable and not criminal under
any of the following circumstances:

1. A parent or guardian and a teacher or other person entrusted
with the care and supervision of a minor or incompetent person may use
reasonable and appropriate physical force upon the minor or incompetent
person when and to the extent reasonably necessary and appropriate to
maintain discipline.
2. A superintendent or other entrusted official of a jail, prison
or correctional institution may use physical force for the preservation
of peace, to maintain order or discipline, or to prevent the commission
of any felony or misdemeanor.
3. A person responsible for the maintenance of order in a place
where others are assembled or on a common motor carrier of passengers, or
a person acting under his direction, may use physical force if and to the
extent that a reasonable person would believe it necessary to maintain
order, but such person may use deadly physical force only if reasonably
necessary to prevent death or serious physical injury.
4. A person acting under a reasonable belief that another person
is about to commit suicide or to inflict serious physical injury upon
himself may use physical force upon that person to the extent reasonably
necessary to thwart the result.
5. A duly licensed physician or a registered nurse or a person
acting under his direction, or any other person who renders emergency
care at the scene of an emergency occurrence, may use reasonable physical
force for the purpose of administering a recognized and lawful form of
treatment which is reasonably adapted to promoting the physical or
mental health of the patient if:

(a) The treatment is administered with the consent of the patient or, if the patient is a minor or an incompetent person, with the consent of his parent, guardian or other person entrusted with his care and supervision except as otherwise provided by law; or

(b) The treatment is administered in an emergency when the person administering such treatment reasonably believes that no one competent to consent can be consulted and that a reasonable person, wishing to safeguard the welfare of the patient, would consent.

6. A person may otherwise use physical force upon another person as further provided in this chapter.

13-404. Justification; self-defense

A. Except as provided in subsection B of this section, a person is justified in threatening or using physical force against another when and to the extent a reasonable person would believe that physical force is immediately necessary to protect himself against the other's use or attempted use of unlawful physical force.

B. The threat or use of physical force against another is not justified:

1. In response to verbal provocation alone; or

2. To resist an arrest that the person knows or should know is being made by a peace officer or by a person acting in a peace officer's presence and at his direction, whether the arrest is lawful or unlawful, unless the physical force used by the peace officer exceeds that allowed by law; or

3. If the person provoked the other's use or attempted use of unlawful physical force, unless:

(a) The person withdraws from the encounter or clearly communicates to the other his intent to do so reasonably believing he cannot safely withdraw from the encounter; and

(b) The other nevertheless continues or attempts to use unlawful physical force against the person.

13-405. Justification; use of deadly physical force

A person is justified in threatening or using deadly physical force against another:

1. If such person would be justified in threatening or using physical force against the other under section 13-404, and

2. When and to the degree a reasonable person would believe that deadly physical force is immediately necessary to protect himself against the other's use or attempted use of unlawful deadly physical force.

13-406. Justification; defense of a third person

A person is justified in threatening or using physical force or deadly physical force against another to protect a third person if:

1. Under the circumstances as a reasonable person would believe them to be, such person would be justified under section 13-404 or 13-405 in threatening or using physical force or deadly physical force to protect himself against the unlawful physical force or deadly physical force a reasonable person would believe is threatening the third person he seeks to protect; and

2. A reasonable person would believe that such person's intervention is immediately necessary to protect the third person.

13-407. Justification; use of physical force in defense of premises

A. A person or his agent in lawful possession or control of premises is justified in threatening to use deadly physical force or in threatening or using physical force against another when and to the extent that a reasonable person would believe it immediately necessary

to prevent or terminate the commission or attempted commission of a
criminal trespass by the other person in or upon the premises.
    B. A person may use deadly physical force under subsection A only
in the defense of himself or third persons as described in sections
13-405 and 13-406.
    C. In this section, "premises" means any real property and any
structure, movable or immovable, permanent or temporary, adapted for
both human residence and lodging whether occupied or not.

13-408. Justification; use of physical force in defense of property

    A person is justified in using physical force against another when
and to the extent that a reasonable person would believe it necessary to
prevent what a reasonable person would believe is an attempt or
commission by the other person of theft or criminal damage involving
tangible movable property under his possession or control, but such
person may use deadly physical force under these circumstances as
provided in sections 13-405, 13-406 and 13-411.

13-409. Justification; use of physical force in law enforcement

    A person is justified in threatening or using physical force
against another if in making or assisting in making an arrest or
detention or in preventing or assisting in preventing the escape after
arrest or detention of that other person, such person uses or threatens
to use physical force and all of the following exist:
    1. A reasonable person would believe that such force is
immediately necessary to effect the arrest or detention or prevent the
escape.
    2. Such person makes known the purpose of the arrest or detention
or believes that it is otherwise known or cannot reasonably be made known
to the person to be arrested or detained.
    3. A reasonable person would believe the arrest or detention to
be lawful.

13-410. Justification; use of deadly physical force in law enforcement

    A. The threatened use of deadly physical force by a person against
another is justified pursuant to section 13-409 only if a reasonable
person effecting the arrest or preventing the escape would believe
the suspect or escapee is:
    1. Actually resisting the discharge of a legal duty with deadly
physical force or with the apparent capacity to use deadly physical
force; or
    2. A felon who has escaped from lawful confinement; or
    3. A felon who is fleeing from justice or resisting arrest with
physical force.
    B. The use of deadly physical force by a person other than a
peace officer against another is justified pursuant to section 13-409
only if a reasonable person effecting the arrest or preventing the
escape would believe the suspect or escapee is actually resisting the
discharge of a legal duty with physical force or with the apparent
capacity to use deadly physical force.

13-411. Justification; use of force in crime prevention

    A. A person is justified in threatening or using both physical
force and deadly physical force against another if and to the extent the
person reasonably believes that physical force or deadly physical force
is immediately necessary to prevent the other's commission of arson of an
occupied structure under section 13-1704, burglary in the second or
first degree under section 13-1507 or 13-1508, kidnapping under section
13-1304, manslaughter under section 13-1103, second or first degree
murder under section 13-1104 or 13-1105, sexual conduct with a minor
under section 13-1405, sexual assault under section 13-1406, child
molestation under section 13-1410, armed robbery under section 13-1904,

or aggravated assault under section 13-1204, subsection A, paragraphs 1 and 2.

B.   There is no duty to retreat before threatening or using deadly physical force justified by subsection A of this section.

C.   A person is presumed to be acting reasonably for the purposes of this section if he is acting to prevent the commission of any of the offenses listed in subsection A of this section.

13-412. Duress

A.   Conduct which would otherwise constitute an offense is justified if a reasonable person would believe that he was compelled to engage in the proscribed conduct by the threat or use of immediate physical force against his person or the person of another which resulted or could result in serious physical injury which a reasonable person in the situation would not have resisted.

B.   The defense provided by subsection A is unavailable if the person intentionally, knowingly or recklessly placed himself in a situation in which it was probable that he would be subjected to duress.

C.   The defense provided by subsection A is unavailable for offenses involving homicide or serious physical injury.

13-413. No civil liability for justified conduct

No person in this state shall be subject to civil liability for engaging in conduct otherwise justified pursuant to the provisions of this chapter.

CHAPTER 5

RESPONSIBILITY

13-501. Immaturity

A person less than fourteen years old at the time of the conduct charged is not criminally responsible in the absence of clear proof that at the time of committing the conduct charged the person knew it was wrong.

CHAPTER 6

CLASSIFICATIONS OF OFFENSES AND AUTHORIZED
DISPOSITIONS OF OFFENDERS

13-601. Classification of offenses

A.   Felonies are classified, for the purpose of sentence, into the following six categories:

1. Class 1 felonies.
2. Class 2 felonies.
3. Class 3 felonies.
4. Class 4 felonies.
5. Class 5 felonies.
6. Class 6 felonies.

B.   Misdemeanors are classified, for the purpose of sentence, into the following three categories:

1. Class 1 misdemeanors.
2. Class 2 misdemeanors.
3. Class 3 misdemeanors.

C.   Petty offenses are not classified.

13-602. Designation of offenses

A.   The particular classification of each felony defined in this title is expressly designated in the section or chapter defining it. Any offense defined outside this title which is declared by law to be a felony without either specification of the classification or of the penalty is a class 5 felony.

B. The particular classification of each misdemeanor defined in this title is expressly designated in the section or chapter defining it. Any offense defined outside this title which is declared by law to be a misdemeanor without either specification of the classification or of the penalty is a class 2 misdemeanor.

C. Every petty offense in this title is expressly designated as such. Any offense defined outside this title without either designation as a felony or misdemeanor or specification of the classification or the penalty is a petty offense.

CHAPTER 7

IMPRISONMENT

13-701. Sentence of imprisonment for felony; presentence report

A. A sentence of imprisonment for a felony shall be a definite term of years and the person sentenced, unless otherwise provided by law, shall be committed to the custody of the state department of corrections.

B. No prisoner may be transferred to the custody of the state department of corrections without a certified copy of the judgment and sentence, signed by the sentencing judge, and a copy of a recent presentence investigation report unless the court has waived preparation of the report.

C. Except as provided in section 13-604 the term of imprisonment for a felony shall be determined as follows for a first offense:

1. For a class 2 felony, seven years.
2. For a class 3 felony, five years.
3. For a class 4 felony, four years.
4. For a class 5 felony, two years.
5. For a class 6 felony, one and one-half years.

13-702. Sentencing

A. Sentences provided in section 13-701 for a first conviction of a class 4, 5 or 6 felony, except those felonies involving a use or exhibition of a deadly weapon or dangerous instrument or when the intentional or knowing infliction of serious physical injury upon another has occurred, may be increased by the court up to twenty-five per cent or may be reduced by the court up to fifty per cent of the sentence prescribed for said offense. Such reduction or increase shall be based on the aggravating and mitigating circumstances contained in subsections D and E of this section.

B. Sentences provided in section 13-701 for a first conviction of a class 2 or 3 felony, except those felonies involving a use or exhibition of a deadly weapon or dangerous instrument or when the intentional or knowing infliction of serious physical injury upon another has occurred, may be increased by the court up to one hundred per cent or may be reduced by the court up to twenty-five per cent of the sentence prescribed for said offense. Such reduction or increase shall be based on aggravating and mitigating circumstances contained in subsections D and E of this section.

CHAPTER 8

RESTITUTION AND FINES

13-801. Fines for felonies

A. A sentence to pay a fine for a felony shall be a sentence to pay an amount fixed by the court not more than one hundred fifty thousand dollars.

B. A judgment that the defendant shall pay a fine, with or without the alternative of imprisonment, shall constitute a lien in like manner as a judgment for money rendered in a civil action.

C. This section does not apply to an enterprise.

13-802. Fines for misdemeanors
A. A sentence to pay a fine for a class 1 misdemeanor shall be a sentence to pay an amount, fixed by the court, not more than one thousand dollars.
B. A sentence to pay a fine for a class 2 misdemeanor shall be a sentence to pay an amount, fixed by the court, not more than seven hundred fifty dollars.
C. A sentence to pay a fine for a class 3 misdemeanor shall be a sentence to pay an amount, fixed by the court, not more than five hundred dollars.
D. A sentence to pay a fine for a petty offense shall be a sentence to pay an amount, fixed by the court, of not more than three hundred dollars.
E. A judgment that the defendant shall pay a fine, with or without the alternative of imprisonment, shall constitute a lien in like manner as a judgment for money rendered in a civil action.
F. This section does not apply to an enterprise.

13-803. Fines against enterprises
A. A sentence to pay a fine, imposed on an enterprise for an offense defined in this title or for an offense defined outside this title for which no special enterprise fine is specified, shall be a sentence to pay an amount, fixed by the court, of not more than:
1. For a felony, one million dollars.
2. For a class 1 misdemeanor, twenty thousand dollars.
3. For a class 2 misdemeanor, ten thousand dollars.
4. For a class 3 misdemeanor, two thousand dollars.
5. For a petty offense, one thousand dollars.
B. A judgment that the enterprise shall pay a fine shall constitute a lien in like manner as a judgment for money rendered in a civil action.

CHAPTER 11

HOMICIDE

13-1101. Definitions
In this chapter, unless the context otherwise requires:
1. "Premeditation" means that the defendant acts with either the intention or the knowledge that he will kill another human being, when such intention or knowledge precedes the killing by a length of time to permit reflection. An act is not done with premeditation if it is the instant effect of a sudden quarrel or heat of passion.
2. "Homicide" means first degree murder, second degree murder, manslaughter or negligent homicide.
3. "Person" means a human being.
4. "Adequate provocation" means conduct or circumstances sufficient to deprive a reasonable person of self-control.

13-1102. Negligent homicide; classification
A. A person commits negligent homicide if with criminal negligence such person causes the death of another person.
B. Negligent homicide is a class 4 felony.

13-1103. Manslaughter; classification
A. A person commits manslaughter by:
1. Recklessly causing the death of another person; or
2. Committing second degree murder as defined in section 13-1104, subsection A upon a sudden quarrel or heat of passion resulting from adequate provocation by the victim; or
3. Intentionally aiding another to commit suicide; or
4. Committing second degree murder as defined in section 13-1104, subsection A, paragraph 3, while being coerced to do so by the use or

threatened immediate use of unlawful deadly physical force upon such person or a third person which a reasonable person in his situation would have been unable to resist; or

5. Knowingly or recklessly causing the death of an unborn child at any stage of its development by any physical injury to the mother of such child which would be murder if the death of the mother had occurred.

B. Manslaughter is a class 3 felony.

13-1104. Second degree murder; classification

A. A person commits second degree murder if without premeditation:

1. Such person intentionally causes the death of another person; or

2. Knowing that his conduct will cause death or serious physical injury, such person causes the death of another person; or

3. Under circumstances manifesting extreme indifference to human life, such person recklessly engages in conduct which creates a grave risk of death and thereby causes the death of another person.

B. Second degree murder is a class 1 felony and is punishable as provided by section 13-604, subsection N, section 13-604.01 if the victim is under fifteen years of age or section 13-710.

13-1105. First degree murder; classification

A. A person commits first degree murder if:

1. Intending or knowing that his conduct will cause death, such person causes the death of another with premeditation; or

2. Acting either alone or with one or more other persons such person commits or attempts to commit sexual conduct with a minor under section 13-1405, sexual assault under section 13-1406, molestation of a child under section 13-1410, narcotics offenses under section 13-3408, subsection A, paragraph 7 or section 13-3409, kidnapping under section 13-1304, burglary under section 13-1506, 13-1507 or 13-1508, arson of an occupied structure under section 13-1704, robbery under section 13-1902, 13-1903 or 13-1904, escape under section 13-2503 or 13-2504 or child abuse under section 13-3623, subsection B, paragraph 1, and in the course of and in furtherance of such offense or immediate flight from such offense, such person or another person causes the death of any person.

B. Homicide, as defined in subsection A, paragraph 2 of this section, requires no specific mental state other than what is required for the commission of any of the enumerated felonies.

C. First degree murder is a class 1 felony and is punishable by death or life imprisonment as provided by section 13-703.

CHAPTER 12

ASSAULT AND RELATED OFFENSES

13-1201. Endangerment; classification

A. A person commits endangerment by recklessly endangering another person with a substantial risk of imminent death or physical injury.

B. Endangerment involving a substantial risk of imminent death is a class 6 felony. In all other cases, it is a class 1 misdemeanor.

13-1202. Threatening or intimidating; classification

A. A person commits threatening or intimidating if such person with the intent to terrify threatens or intimidates by word or conduct:

1. To cause physical injury to another person or serious damage to property of another; or

2. To cause, or in reckless disregard to causing, serious public inconvenience including, but not limited to, evacuation of a building, place of assembly, or transportation facility.

B.   Threatening or intimidating is a class 1 misdemeanor.

13-1203. Assault; classification
A.   A person commits assault by:
1.   Intentionally, knowingly or recklessly causing any physical injury to another person; or
2.   Intentionally placing another person in reasonable apprehension of imminent physical injury; or
3.   Knowingly touching another person with the intent to injure, insult or provoke such person.
B.   Assault committed intentionally or knowingly pursuant to subsection A, paragraph 1 is a class 1 misdemeanor. Assault committed recklessly pursuant to subsection A, paragraph 1 or assault pursuant to subsection A, paragraph 2 is a class 2 misdemeanor. Assault committed pursuant to subsection A, paragraph 3 is a class 3 misdemeanor.

13-1204. Aggravated assault; classification
A.   A person commits aggravated assault if such person commits assault as defined in section 13-1203 under any of the following circumstances:
1.   If such person causes serious physical injury to another.
2.   If such person uses a deadly weapon or dangerous instrument.
3.   If such person commits the assault after entering the private home of another with the intent to commit the assault.
4.   If such person is eighteen years of age or more and commits the assault upon a child the age of fifteen years or under.
5.   If such person commits the assault knowing or having reason to know that the victim is a peace officer, or a person summoned and directed by such officer while engaged in the execution of any official duties.
6.   If such person commits the assault knowing or having reason to know the victim is a teacher or other person employed by any school and such teacher or other employee is upon the grounds of a school or grounds adjacent to such school or is in any part of a building or vehicle used for school purposes, or any teacher or school nurse visiting a private home in the course of his professional duties, or any teacher engaged in any authorized and organized classroom activity held on other than school grounds.
7.   If such person is imprisoned in the custody of the department of corrections, a law enforcement agency, county or city jail, or adult or juvenile detention facility of a city or county or subject to the custody of personnel from such department, agency, jail or detention facility and commits the assault knowing or having reason to know the victim is an employee of such department, agency, jail or detention facility acting in an official capacity.
8.   If such person commits the assault while the victim is bound or otherwise physically restrained or while the victim's capacity to resist is substantially impaired.
B.   Aggravated assault pursuant to subsection A, paragraph 1 or 2 of this section is a class 3 felony except if the victim is under fifteen years of age in which case it is a class 2 felony punishable pursuant to section 13-604.01. Aggravated assault pursuant to subsection A, paragraph 7 of this section is a class 5 felony. Aggravated assault pursuant to subsection A, paragraph 3, 4, 5, 6 or 8 of this section is a class 6 felony.

CHAPTER 13

KIDNAPPING AND RELATED OFFFENSES

13-1304. Kidnapping; classification; consecutive sentence
A. A person commits kidnapping by knowingly restraining another person with the intent to:
1. Hold the victim for ransom, as a shield or hostage; or
2. Hold the victim for involuntary servitude; or
3. Inflict death, physical injury or a sexual offense on the victim, or to otherwise aid in the commission of a felony; or
4. Place the victim or a third person in reasonable apprehension of imminent physical injury to the victim or such third person.
5. Interfere with the performance of a governmental or political function.
6. Seize or exercise control over any airplane, train, bus, ship or other vehicle.
B. Kidnapping is a class 2 felony unless the victim is released voluntarily by the defendant without physical injury in a safe place prior to arrest and prior to accomplishing any of the further enumerated offenses in subsection A of this section in which case it is a class 4 felony. If the victim is released pursuant to an agreement with the state and without any physical injury, it is a class 3 felony. If the victim is under fifteen years of age kidnapping is a class 2 felony punishable pursuant to section 13-604.01. The sentence for kidnapping of a victim under fifteen years of age shall run consecutively to any other sentence imposed on the defendant and to any undischarged term of imprisonment of the defendant.

CHAPTER 14

SEXUAL OFFENSES

13-1405. Sexual conduct with a minor; classifications
A. A person commits sexual conduct with a minor by intentionally or knowingly engaging in sexual intercourse or oral sexual contact with any person who is under eighteen years of age.
B. Sexual conduct with a minor under fifteen years of age is a class 2 felony and is punishable pursuant to section 13-604.01. Sexual conduct with a minor fifteen years of age or over is a class 6 felony.

13-1406. Sexual assault; classifications
A. A person commits sexual assault by intentionally or knowingly engaging in sexual intercourse or oral sexual contact with any person without consent of such person.
B. Sexual assault of a person fifteen years of age or older is a class 2 felony, and the person convicted is not eligible for suspension or commutation of sentence, probation, pardon, parole, work furlough or release from confinement on any other basis except as specifically authorized by section 31-233, subsection A or B until the sentence imposed by the court has been served. If the victim is under fifteen years of age, sexual assault is a class 2 felony and is punishable pursuant to section 13-604.01.

13-1410. Molestation of child; classification
A person who knowingly molests a child under the age of fifteen years by directly or indirectly touching the private parts of such child or who causes a child under the age of fifteen years to directly or indirectly touch the private parts of such person is guilty of a class 2 felony and is punishable pursuant to section 13-604.01.

CHAPTER 15

CRIMINAL TRESPASS AND BURGLARY

13-1502. Criminal trespass in the third degree; classification
A. A person commits criminal trespass in the third degree by:
1. Knowingly entering or remaining unlawfully on any real property after a reasonable request to leave by the owner or any other person having lawful control over such property, or reasonable notice prohibiting entry.
2. Knowingly entering or remaining unlawfully on the right-of-way for tracks, or the storage or switching yards or rolling stock of a railroad company.
B. Criminal trespass in the third degree is a class 3 misdemeanor.

13-1503. Criminal trespass in the second degree; classification
A. A person commits criminal trespass in the second degree by knowingly entering or remaining unlawfully in or on any nonresidential structure or in any fenced commercial yard.
B. Criminal trespass in the second degree is a class 2 misdemeanor.

13-1504. Criminal trespass in the first degree; classification
A. A person commits criminal trespass in the first degree by knowingly:
1. Entering or remaining unlawfully in or on a residential structure or in a fenced residential yard; or
2. Entering any residential yard and, without lawful authority, looking into the residential structure thereon in reckless disregard of infringing on the inhabitant's right of privacy.
3. Entering unlawfully on real property subject to a valid mineral claim or lease with the intent to hold, work, take or explore for minerals on such claim or lease.
4. Entering or remaining unlawfully on the property of another and burning, defacing, mutilating or otherwise desecrating a religious symbol or other religious property of another without the express permission of the owner of the property.
B. Criminal trespass in the first degree is a class 6 felony if it is committed by entering or remaining unlawfully in or on a residential structure or committed pursuant to subsection A, paragraph 4. Criminal trespass in the first degree is a class 1 misdemeanor if it is committed by entering or remaining unlawfully in a fenced residential yard or committed pursuant to subsection A, paragraph 2 or 3.

13-1506. Burglary in the third degree; classification
A. A person commits burglary in the third degree by entering or remaining unlawfully in or on a nonresidential structure or in a fenced commercial or residential yard with the intent to commit any theft or any felony therein.
B. Burglary in the third degree is a class 4 felony.

13-1507. Burglary in the second degree; classification
A. A person commits burglary in the second degree by entering or remaining unlawfully in or on a residential structure with the intent to commit any theft or any felony therein.
B. Burglary in the second degree is a class 3 felony.

13-1508. Burglary in the first degree; classification
A. A person commits burglary in the first degree if such person or an accomplice violates the provisions of either section 13-1506 or 13-1507 and knowingly possesses explosives, a deadly weapon or a

dangerous instrument in the course of committing any theft or any felony.

B. Burglary in the first degree of a nonresidential structure or a fenced commercial or residential yard is a class 3 felony. It is a class 2 felony if committed in a residential structure.

CHAPTER 17

ARSON

13-1704. Arson of an occupied structure; classification

A. A person commits arson of an occupied structure by knowingly and unlawfully damaging an occupied structure by knowingly causing a fire or explosion.

B. Arson of an occupied structure is a class 2 felony.

CHAPTER 19

ROBBERY

13-1904. Armed robbery; classification

A. A person commits armed robbery if, in the course of committing robbery as defined in section 13-1902, such person or an accomplice:

1. Is armed with a deadly weapon or a simulated deadly weapon; or

2. Uses or threatens to use a deadly weapon or dangerous instrument or a simulated deadly weapon.

B. Armed robbery is a class 2 felony.

CHAPTER 24

OBSTRUCTION OF PUBLIC ADMINISTRATION

13-2403. Refusing to aid a peace officer; classification

A. A person commits refusing to aid a peace officer if, upon a reasonable command by a person reasonably known to be a peace officer, such person knowingly refuses or fails to aid such peace officer in:

1. Effectuating or securing an arrest; or

2. Preventing the commission by another of any offense.

B. A person who complies with this section by aiding a peace officer shall not be held liable to any person for damages resulting therefrom, provided such person acted reasonably under the circumstances known to him at the time.

C. Refusing to aid a peace officer is a class 1 misdemeanor.

13-2409. Obstructing criminal investigations or prosecutions; classification

A person who knowingly attempts by means of bribery, misrepresentation, intimidation or force or threats of force to obstruct, delay or prevent the communication of information or testimony relating to a violation of any criminal statute to a peace officer, magistrate, prosecutor or grand jury or who knowingly injures another in his person or property on account of the giving by the latter or by any other person of any such information or testimony to a peace officer, magistrate, prosecutor or grand jury is guilty of a class 5 felony.

CHAPTER 25

ESCAPE AND RELATED OFFENSES

13-2502. Escape in the third degree; classification

A. A person commits escape in the third degree if, having been arrested for, charged with or found guilty of a misdemeanor or petty offense, such person knowingly escapes or attempts to escape from custody.

B. Escape in the third degree is a class 6 felony.

13-2503. Escape in the second degree; classification
A. A person commits escape in the second degree by knowingly:
1. Escaping or attempting to escape from a correctional facility; or
2. Escaping or attempting to escape from custody imposed as a result of having been arrested for, charged with or found guilty of a felony.
B. Escape in the second degree is a class 5 felony and the sentence imposed for a violation of this section shall run consecutively to any sentence of imprisonment for which the defendant was confined or to any term of conditional release from the sentence including probation, parole, work furlough or any other release.

13-2504. Escape in the first degree; classification
A. A person commits escape in the first degree by knowingly escaping or attempting to escape from custody or a correctional facility by:
1. Using or threatening the use of physical force against another person; or
2. Using or threatening to use a deadly weapon or dangerous instrument against another person.
B. Escape in the first degree is a class 4 felony and the sentence imposed for a violation of this section shall run consecutively to any sentence of imprisonment for which the defendant was confined or to any term of conditional release from the sentence including probation, parole, work furlough or any other release.

13-2505. Promoting prison contraband; definitions; classification
A. A person, not otherwise authorized by law, commits promoting prison contraband:
1. By knowingly taking contraband into a correctional facility or the grounds of such facility; or
2. By knowingly conveying contraband to any person confined in a correctional facility; or
3. By knowingly making, obtaining or possessing contraband while being confined in a correctional facility.
B. Any person who has reasonable grounds to believe there has been a violation or attempted violation of this section shall immediately report such violation or attempted violation to the official in charge of the facility or to a peace officer.
C. Promoting prison contraband if the contraband is a deadly weapon, dangerous instrument or explosive is a class 2 felony. Promoting prison contraband if the contraband is a dangerous drug, narcotic drug or marijuana is a class 2 felony. In all other cases promoting prison contraband is a class 5 felony. Failure to report a violation or attempted violation of this section is a class 5 felony.

13-2508. Resisting arrest; classification
A. A person commits resisting arrest by intentionally preventing or attempting to prevent a person reasonably known to him to be a peace officer, acting under color of such peace officer's official authority, from effecting an arrest by:
1. Using or threatening to use physical force against the peace officer or another; or
2. Using any other means creating a substantial risk of causing physical injury to the peace officer or another.
B. Resisting arrest is a class 6 felony.

13-2510. Hindering prosecution; definition
For purposes of sections 13-2511 and 13-2512 a person renders assistance to another person by knowingly:
1. Harboring or concealing the other person; or

2. Warning the other person of impending discovery, apprehension, prosecution or conviction. This does not apply to a warning given in connection with an effort to bring another into compliance with the law; or

3. Providing the other person with money, transportation, a weapon, a disguise or other similar means of avoiding discovery, apprehension, prosecution or conviction; or

4. Preventing or obstructing by means of force, deception or intimidation anyone from performing an act that might aid in the discovery, apprehension, prosecution or conviction of the other person; or

5. Suppressing by an act of concealment, alteration or destruction any physical evidence that might aid in the discovery, apprehension, prosecution or conviction of the other person; or

6. Concealing the identity of the other person.

13-2511. Hindering prosecution in the second degree; classification
A. A person commits hindering prosecution in the second degree if, with the intent to hinder the apprehension, prosecution, conviction or punishment of another for any misdemeanor or petty offense, such person renders assistance to such person.
B. Hindering prosecution in the second degree is a class 1 misdemeanor.

13-2512. Hindering prosecution in the first degree; classification
A. A person commits hindering prosecution in the first degree if, with the intent to hinder the apprehension, prosecution, conviction or punishment of another for any felony, such person renders assistance to such person.
B. Hindering prosecution in the first degree is a class 5 felony.

CHAPTER 27

PERJURY AND RELATED OFFENSES

13-2702. Perjury; classification
A. A person commits perjury by making a false sworn statement in regard to a material issue, believing it to be false.
B. Perjury is a class 4 felony.

CHAPTER 28

INTERFERENCE WITH JUDICIAL AND OTHER PROCEEDINGS

13-2809. Tampering with physical evidence; classification
A. A person commits tampering with physical evidence if, with intent that it be used, introduced, rejected or unavailable in an official proceeding which is then pending or which such person knows is about to be instituted, such person:
1. Destroys, mutilates, alters, conceals or removes physical evidence with the intent to impair its verity or availability; or
2. Knowingly makes, produces or offers any false physical evidence; or
3. Prevents the production of physical evidence by an act of force, intimidation or deception against any person.
B. Inadmissibility of the evidence in question is not a defense.
C. Tampering with physical evidence is a class 6 felony.

CHAPTER 29

OFFENSES AGAINST PUBLIC ORDER

13-2904. Disorderly conduct; classification

A. A person commits disorderly conduct if, with intent to disturb the peace or quiet of a neighborhood, family or person, or with knowledge of doing so, such person:

1. Engages in fighting, violent or seriously disruptive behavior; or

2. Makes unreasonable noise; or

3. Uses abusive or offensive language or gestures to any person present in a manner likely to provoke immediate physical retaliation by such person; or

4. Makes any protracted commotion, utterance or display with the intent to prevent the transaction of the business of a lawful meeting, gathering or procession; or

5. Refuses to obey a lawful order to disperse issued to maintain public safety in dangerous proximity to a fire, hazard or other emergency; or

6. Recklessly handles, displays or discharges a deadly weapon or dangerous instrument.

B. Disorderly conduct is a class 1 misdemeanor.

13-2908. Criminal nuisance; classification

A. A person commits criminal nuisance:

1. If, by conduct either unlawful in itself or unreasonable under the circumstances, such person recklessly creates or maintains a condition which endangers the safety or health of others.

2. By knowingly conducting or maintaining any premises, place or resort where persons gather for purposes of engaging in unlawful conduct.

B. Criminal nuisance is a class 3 misdemeanor.

13-2911. Interference with the peaceful conduct of educational institutions; definitions; violation; classification

A. A person commits interference with the peaceful conduct of educational institutions by knowingly:

1. Going upon or remaining upon the property of any educational institution in violation of any rule of such institution or for the purpose of interfering with the lawful use of such property by others or in such manner as to deny or interfere with the lawful use of such property by others; or

2. Refusing to obey a lawful order given pursuant to subsection B of this section.

B. When the chief administrative officer of an educational institution or an officer or employee designated by him to maintain order has reasonable grounds to believe that any person or persons are committing any act which interferes with or disrupts the lawful use of such property by others at the educational institution or has reasonable grounds to believe any person has entered upon the property for the purpose of committing such an act, such officer or employee may order such person to leave the property of the educational institution.

C. The appropriate governing board of every educational institution shall adopt rules for the maintenance of public order upon all property under its jurisdiction which is used for educational purposes and shall provide a program for the enforcement of such rules. Such rules shall govern the conduct of students, faculty and other staff and all members of the public while on the property. Penalties for violations of such rules shall be clearly set forth and enforced. Penalties shall include provisions for the ejection of a violator from the property and, in the case of a student, faculty member or other staff violator, his suspension, expulsion or other appropriate disciplinary action. Adoption of all rules required by this section shall be governed by title 41, chapter 6, and such rules shall be amended as necessary to ensure the maintenance of public order. Any deadly weapon, dangerous instrument or explosive used, displayed or possessed by a person in violation of a rule adopted pursuant to this subsection shall be forfeited and sold, destroyed, or otherwise disposed of according to chapter 39 of this title. Nothing in this subsection shall preclude school districts from conducting approved gun safety programs on school campuses. This subsection shall not apply to private universities, colleges, high schools or common schools or other private educational institutions.

H. Interference with the peaceful conduct of educational institutions is a class 1 misdemeanor.

CHAPTER 31

WEAPONS AND EXPLOSIVES

13-3101. Definitions

In this chapter, unless the context otherwise requires:

1. "Deadly weapon" means anything designed for lethal use. The term includes a firearm.

2. "Deface" means to remove, alter or destroy the manufacturer's serial number.

3. "Explosive" means any dynamite, nitroglycerine, black powder or other similar explosive material including plastic explosives but does not mean or include ammunition or ammunition components such as primers, percussion caps, smokeless powder, black powder and black powder substitutes used for hand loading purposes.

4. "Firearm" means any loaded or unloaded pistol, revolver, rifle, shotgun or other weapon which will or is designed to or may readily be converted to expel a projectile by the action of an explosive, except that it does not include a firearm in permanently inoperable condition.

5. "Prohibited possessor" means any person:

(a) Who has been found to constitute a danger to himself or to others pursuant to court order under the provisions of section 36-540, and whose court ordered treatment has not been terminated by court order.

(b) Who has been convicted within or without this state of a felony involving violence or possession and use of a deadly weapon or dangerous instrument and whose civil rights have not been restored.

(c) Who is at the time of possession serving a term of imprisonment in any correctional or detention facility.

6. "Prohibited weapon" means, but does not include, fireworks imported, distributed or used in compliance with state laws or local ordinances, any propellant, propellant actuated devices or propellant actuated industrial tools which are manufactured, imported or distributed for their intended purposes or a device which is commercially manufactured primarily for the purpose of illumination, any:

(a) Explosive, incendiary or poison gas:

(i) Bomb.

(ii) Grenade.

(iii) Rocket having a propellant charge of more than four ounces.

(iv) Mine.

(b) Device designed, made or adapted to muffle the report of a firearm; or

(c) Firearm that is capable of shooting more than one shot automatically, without manual reloading, by a single function of the trigger; or

(d) Rifle with a barrel length of less than sixteen inches, or shotgun with a barrel length of less than eighteen inches, or any firearm made from a rifle or shotgun which, as modified, has an overall length of less than twenty-six inches; or

(e) Instrument, including a nunchaku, that consists of two or more sticks, clubs, bars or rods to be used as handles, connected by a rope, cord, wire or chain, in the design of a weapon used in connection with the practice of a system of self-defense; or

(f) Breakable container which contains a flammable liquid with a flash point of one hundred fifty degrees fahrenheit or less and has a wick or similar device capable of being ignited; or

(g) Combination of parts or materials designed and intended for use in making or converting a device into an item set forth in subdivision (a) or (f) of this paragraph.

The items as set forth in subdivisions (a), (b), (c) and (d) of this paragraph shall not include any such firearms or devices registered in the national firearms registry and transfer records of the United States treasury department or any firearm which has been classified as a curio or relic by the United States treasury department.

Section 13-3102, Arizona Revised Statutes, was amended by Laws 1991, chapter 237, section 1 and Laws 1991, chapter 316, section 3. These two versions could not be blended because the chapter 316 version failed to conform an internal reference in subsection C. To accomplish the intent of these enactments, in this act the Laws 1991, chapter 237 version of section 13-3102, Arizona Revised Statutes, is amended to conform the internal reference in subsection C and to incorporate the amendments made by Laws 1991, chapter 316 and the chapter 316 version is repealed.

Sec. __. Section 13-3102, Arizona Revised Statutes, as amended by Laws 1991, chapter 237, section 1, is amended to read:
13-3102. Misconduct involving weapons; defenses; classification; definitions
A. A person commits misconduct involving weapons by knowingly:
1. Carrying a deadly weapon except a pocket knife concealed on his person; or
2. Carrying a deadly weapon concealed within immediate control of any person in or on a means of transportation; or
3. Manufacturing, possessing, transporting, selling or transferring a prohibited weapon; or
4. Possessing a deadly weapon if such person is a prohibited possessor; or
5. Selling or transferring a deadly weapon to a prohibited possessor; or
6. Defacing a deadly weapon; or
7. Possessing a defaced deadly weapon knowing the deadly weapon was defaced; or
8. Using or possessing a deadly weapon during the commission of any felony offense included in chapter 34 of this title; or
9. DISCHARGING A FIREARM AT AN OCCUPIED STRUCTURE IN ORDER TO ASSIST, PROMOTE OR FURTHER THE INTERESTS OF A CRIMINAL STREET GANG, A CRIMINAL SYNDICATE OR A RACKETEERING ENTERPRISE WHEN SUCH CONDUCT DOES NOT RESULT IN THE DEATH OR PHYSICAL INJURY OF ANOTHER PERSON; OR
9̶.̶ 10. Unless specifically authorized by law, entering any public establishment or attending any public event and carrying a deadly weapon on his person after a reasonable request by the operator of the establishment or the sponsor of the event or his agent to remove his weapon and place it in the custody of the operator of the establishment or the sponsor of the event; or
1̶0̶.̶ 11. Unless specifically authorized by law, entering an election polling place on the day of any election carrying a deadly weapon; or
1̶1̶.̶ 12. Possessing a deadly weapon on school grounds.
B. Subsection A, paragraph 1 of this section shall not apply to a person in his dwelling, on his business premises or on real property owned or leased by that person.
C. Subsection A, paragraphs 1, 2, 3, 7, 9̶,̶ 10, a̶n̶d̶ 11 AND 12 of this section shall not apply to:
1. A peace officer or any person summoned by any peace officer to assist and while actually assisting in the performance of official duties; or
2. A member of the military forces of the United States or of any state of the United States in the performance of official duties; or
3. A person specifically licensed, authorized or permitted pursuant to a statute of this state or of the United States.
D. Subsection A, paragraphs 3 and 7 of this section shall not apply to:
1. The p̶o̶s̶s̶e̶s̶s̶i̶o̶n̶ POSSESSING, transporting, selling or transferring of weapons by a museum as a part of its collection or an educational institution for educational purposes or by an authorized employee of such museum or institution, if:

(a) Such museum or institution is operated by the United States or this state or a political subdivision of this state, or by an organization described in section 170(c) of title 26 of the United States Code as a recipient of a charitable contribution; and

(b) Reasonable precautions are taken with respect to theft or misuse of such material.

2. The regular and lawful transporting as merchandise; or

3. Acquisition by a person by operation of law such as by gift, devise or descent or in a fiduciary capacity as a recipient of the property or former property of an insolvent, incapacitated or deceased person.

E. Subsection A, paragraph 3 of this section shall not apply to the merchandise of an authorized manufacturer thereof or dealer therein, when such material is intended to be manufactured, possessed, transported, sold or transferred solely for or to a dealer or a regularly constituted or appointed state, county or municipal police department or police officer, or a detention facility, or the military service of this or another state or the United States, or a museum or educational institution or a person specifically licensed or permitted pursuant to federal or state law.

F. Subsection A, paragraph 1 of this section shall not apply to a weapon or weapons carried in a belt holster which holster is wholly or partially visible, or carried in a scabbard or case designed for carrying weapons which scabbard or case is wholly or partially visible or carried in luggage. Subsection A, paragraph 2 of this section shall not apply to a weapon or weapons carried in a case, holster, scabbard, pack or luggage which are carried within a means of transportation or within a storage compartment, trunk or glove compartment of a means of transportation.

G. Subsection A, paragraph 9— 10 of this section shall not apply to shooting ranges or shooting events, hunting areas or similar locations or activities.

H. Subsection A, paragraph 3 of this section shall not apply to a weapon described in section 13-3101, paragraph 6, subdivision (e), if such weapon is possessed for the purposes of preparing for, conducting or participating in lawful exhibitions, demonstrations, contests or athletic events involving the use of such weapon. Subsection A, paragraph 11 12 of this section shall not apply to a weapon if such weapon is possessed for the purposes of preparing for, conducting or participating in hunter or firearm safety courses.

I. Subsection A, paragraph 11 12 of this section shall not apply to the possession of a:

1. Firearm which is not loaded and which is carried in a locked container within a means of transportation which is not under the control of a pupil.

2. Firearm for use on the school grounds in a program approved by a school.

3. Weapon or weapons carried within a means of transportation when a pupil is being transported to or from school grounds by a parent, guardian, or person, other than the pupil, who is authorized to transport the pupil to or from school grounds.

J. MISCONDUCT INVOLVING WEAPONS UNDER SUBSECTION A, PARAGRAPH 9 OF THIS SECTION IS A CLASS 3 FELONY. Misconduct involving weapons under subsection A, paragraph 3 or 8 of this section is a class 4 felony. Misconduct involving weapons under subsection A, paragraphs 4 through 7 of this section is a class 6 felony. Misconduct involving weapons under subsection A, paragraphs 1, 2, 9, 10, and 11 AND 12 of this section is a class 1 misdemeanor.

K. For purposes of this section:

1. "School" means public or nonpublic kindergarten program, common school or high school.

2. "School grounds" means in, or on the grounds of, a school.

Sec. __. Section 13-3102, Arizona Revised Statutes, as amended by Laws 1991, chapter 316, section 3 is repealed.

13-3103. Misconduct involving explosives; classification

A. A person commits misconduct involving explosives by

knowingly:
1. Keeping or storing a greater quantity than fifty pounds of explosives in or upon any building or premises within a distance of one-half mile of the exterior limits of a city or town, except in vessels, railroad cars or vehicles receiving and keeping them in the course of and for the purpose of transportation; or
2. Keeping or storing percussion caps or any blasting powder within two hundred feet of a building or premises where explosives are kept or stored; or
3. Selling, transporting or possessing explosives without having plainly marked, in a conspicuous place on the box or package containing the explosive, its name, explosive character and date of manufacture.
4. This section shall not apply to any person who legally keeps, stores or transports explosives, percussion caps or blasting powder as a part of their business.
B. Misconduct involving explosives is a class 1 misdemeanor.

13-3104. Depositing explosives; classification
A. A person commits depositing explosives if with the intent to physically endanger, injure, intimidate or terrify any person, such person knowingly deposits any explosive on, in or near any vehicle, building or place where persons inhabit, frequent or assemble.
B. Depositing explosives is a class 4 felony.

13-3105. Forfeiture of weapons and explosives
Upon the conviction of any person for the violation of any felony in this state in which a deadly weapon, dangerous instrument or explosive was used, displayed or unlawfully possessed by such person the court shall order the article forfeited and sold, destroyed or otherwise disposed of in accordance with chapter 39 of this title.

13-3106. Firearm purchase in other states
A person residing in this state, or a corporation or other business entity maintaining a place of business in this state, may purchase or otherwise obtain firearms anywhere in the United States if such purchase or acquisition fully complies with the laws of this state and the state in which the purchase or acquisition is made and the purchaser and seller, prior to the sale or delivery for sale, have complied with all the requirements of the federal gun control act of 1968, public law 90-618, section 922, subsection (c) and the code of federal regulations, volume 26, section 178.96, subsection (c).

13-3107. Control of firearms, hunting and rifle ranges within
             municipalities; classification
A. Discharge of a firearm within the limits of any municipality is a class 2 misdemeanor except:
1. As allowed pursuant to the provisions of chapter 4 of this title.
2. On a properly supervised range.
3. In an area recommended as a hunting area by the Arizona game and fish department, approved and posted as required by the chief of police, but any such area may be closed when deemed unsafe by the chief of police or the director of the game and fish department.
4. For the control of nuisance wildlife by permit from the Arizona game and fish department or the United States fish and wildlife service.
5. By special permit of the chief of police of the municipality.
6. As required by an animal control officer in the performance of duties as specified in section 9-499.04.
B. A properly supervised range for the purposes of this section means a range operated by a club affiliated with the national rifle

association of America, the amateur trapshooting association, the
national skeet association, or any other nationally recognized shooting
organization, any agency of the federal government, state of Arizona,
county or city within which the range is located, or any public or
private school, and, in the case of air or carbon dioxide gas operated
guns, or underground ranges on private or public property, such ranges
may be operated with adult supervision.

13-3108. Firearms regulated by state; state preemption
    A. Ordinances of any political subdivision of this state relating
to the transportation, possession, carrying, sale and use of firearms in
this state shall not be in conflict with this chapter.
    B. A political subdivision of this state shall not require the
licensing or registration of firearms or prohibit the ownership,
purchase, sale or transfer of firearms.

13-3109. Sale or gift of firearm to minor; classification
    A. A person who sells or gives to a minor, without written consent
of the minor's parent or legal guardian, a firearm, ammunition or toy
pistol by which dangerous and explosive substances may be discharged, is
guilty of a class 2 misdemeanor.
    B. Nothing in this section shall be construed to require
reporting sales of firearms, nor shall registration of firearms or
firearms sales be required.

CHAPTER 37

MISCELLANEOUS OFFENSES

13-3708. Introducing a drug, liquor, firearm, weapon or
          explosive into a juvenile correctional institution;
          classification
    A. A person not authorized by law commits introducing a drug,
liquor, firearm, weapon or explosive into a juvenile correctional
institution if such person knowingly brings into a state institution for
juveniles or within the grounds belonging or adjacent to such
institution, any dangerous drug as defined in title 32 or any narcotic
drug as defined in title 36, or intoxicating liquor of any kind, or
firearms, weapons or explosives of any kind.
    B. Introducing a drug, liquor, firearm, weapon or explosive into
a juvenile correctional institution is a class 5 felony.

CHAPTER 38

MISCELLANEOUS

13-3801. Preventing offenses; aiding officer
    A. Public offenses may be prevented by intervention of peace
officers as follows:
    1. By requiring security to keep the peace.
    2. Forming a police detail in cities and towns and requiring
their attendance in exposed places.
    3. Suppressing riots.
    B. When peace officers are authorized to act in preventing public
offenses, other persons, who, by their command, act in their aid, are
justified in so doing.

13-3802. Right to command aid for execution of process;
          punishment for resisting process
    A. When a sheriff or other public officer authorized to execute
process finds, or has reason to believe that resistance will be made to
execution of the process, such officer may command as many inhabitants of
the county as the officer deems proper to assist in overcoming such

resistance.

B. The officer shall certify to the court from which the process issued the names of those persons resisting, and they may be proceeded against for contempt of court.

injury which may have resulted from a fight, brawl, robbery or other illegal or unlawful act, shall immediately notify the chief of police or the city marshal, if in an incorporated city or town, or the sheriff, or the nearest police officer, of the circumstances, together with the name and description of the patient, the character of the wound and other facts which may be of assistance to the police authorities in the event the condition of the patient may be due to any illegal transaction or circumstances.

B. Any violation of the provisions of this section by a physician, surgeon, nurse or hospital attendant, is a class 3 misdemeanor.

13-3884. Arrest by private person

A private person may make an arrest:

1. When the person to be arrested has in his presence committed a misdemeanor amounting to a breach of the peace, or a felony.

2. When a felony has been in fact committed and he has reasonable ground to believe that the person to be arrested has committed it.

13-3889. Method of arrest by private person

A private person when making an arrest shall inform the person to be arrested of the intention to arrest him and the cause of the arrest, unless he is then engaged in the commission of an offense, or is pursued immediately after its commission or after an escape, or flees or forcibly resists before the person making the arrest has opportunity so to inform him, or when the giving of such information will imperil the arrest.

13-3892. Right of private person to break into building

A private person, in order to make an arrest where a felony was committed in his presence, as authorized in section 13-3884, may break open a door or window of any building in which the person to be arrested is or is reasonably believed to be, if he is refused admittance after he has announced his purpose.

13-3893. Right to break door or window to effect release

When an officer or private person has entered a building in accordance with the provisions of section 13-3891 or 13-3892, he may break open a door or window of the building, if detained therein, when necessary for the purpose of liberating himself.

13-3894. Right to break into building in order to effect
            release of person making arrest detained therein

A peace officer or a private person may break open a door or window of any building when necessary for the purpose of liberating a person who entered the building in accordance with the provisions of section 13-3891 or 13-3892 and is detained therein.

13-3895. Weapons to be taken from person arrested

Any person making a lawful arrest may take from the person arrested all weapons which he may have about his person and shall deliver them to the magistrate before whom he is taken.

13-3900. Duty of private person after making arrest

A private person who has made an arrest shall without unnecessary delay take the person arrested before the nearest or most accessible magistrate in the county in which the arrest was made, or deliver him to a peace officer, who shall without unnecessary delay take him before such magistrate. The private person or officer so taking the person arrested before the magistrate shall make before the magistrate a complaint, which shall set forth the facts showing the offense for which the person was arrested. If, however, the officer cannot make the complaint, the private person who delivered the person arrested to the officer shall accompany the officer before the magistrate and shall make to the magistrate the complaint against the person arrested.

13-4305. Seizure of property

A. Property subject to forfeiture under this chapter may be seized for forfeiture by a peace officer:

1. On process issued pursuant to the rules of civil procedure or the provisions of this title including a seizure warrant.

2. By making a seizure for forfeiture on property seized on process issued pursuant to law, including sections 13-3911 through 13-3915.

3. By making a seizure for forfeiture without court process if any of the following is true:

(a) The seizure for forfeiture is of property seized incident to an arrest or search.

(b) The property subject to seizure for forfeiture has been the subject of a prior judgment in favor of this state or any other state or the federal government in a forfeiture proceeding.

(c) The peace officer has probable cause to believe that the property seized for forfeiture is directly or indirectly dangerous to health or safety.

(d) The peace officer has probable cause to believe that the property is subject to forfeiture.

B. In determining probable cause for seizure and for forfeiture, the fact that money or any negotiable instrument was found in proximity to contraband or to instrumentalities of an offense gives rise to an inference that the money or instrument was the proceeds of contraband or was used or intended to be used to facilitate commission of the offense.

ABOUT THE AUTHOR

Alan Korwin is a professional writer and management consultant with 19 years of experience in business, technical, news and promotional communication.

A former editor and a successful businessman, he has a talent for assembling a body of information at its source, and then organizing and presenting it in a way which is clear, effective and enduring.

Mr. Korwin produces technical and business documents, marketing materials, advertising and books for clients ranging from IBM, American Express and AT&T to local merchants and private individuals.

In 1990 he introduced a special training seminar entitled, *Instant Expertise - How To Find Out Practically Anything, Fast.* The 4-hour course reveals trade secrets and shortcuts which professionals use to gather information on anything short of espionage. He also teaches classes on writing, publishing, publicity, and phone power, at Phoenix College, for the City of Scottsdale, and at other locations.